The Power of Poetry for School Leadership

Leading with Attention and Insight

Lystra M. Richardson

A SCARECROWEDUCATION BOOK

The Scarecrow Press, Inc.
Lanham, Maryland, and Oxford
2003

KH

A SCARECROWEDUCATION BOOK

Published in the United States of America
by Scarecrow Press, Inc.
A Member of the Rowman & Littlefield Publishing Group
4501 Forbes Boulevard, Suite 200, Lanham, Maryland 20706
www.scarecroweducation.com

PO Box 317
Oxford
OX2 9RU, UK

British Library Cataloguing in Publication Information Available

Library of Congress Cataloging-in-Publication Data

Richardson, Lystra M., 1954–
  The power of poetry for school leadership : leading with attention and insight
/ Lystra M. Richardson.
     p. cm.
  "A ScarecrowEducation book."
  Includes bibliographical references and index.
  ISBN 0-8108-4708-6 (alk. paper)
  1. Poetry—Study and teaching—United States. 2. Educational
leadership—United States. I. Title.
PN1101.R53 2003
808.1'071'073—dc21

                                                    2002154841

∞™ The paper used in this publication meets the minimum requirements of
American National Standard for Information Sciences—Permanence of
Paper for Printed Library Materials, ANSI/NISO Z39.48-1992.
Manufactured in the United States of America.

10/25/04

To my father, Willis F. Moore (deceased), who did let me know that I would write a book, and to my mother, Hagar Moore, who has provided emotional support so that I could.

Contents

Preface

PURPOSE OF THE BOOK

In times of uncertainty people are primarily concerned with meaning. They tend to intensify the quest for meaning in life and in work. An important area of need in schools is for hands-on tools that can help leaders to create meaning for themselves and those they lead. This book is an attempt to highlight issues of human need in work, particularly in schools, and to suggest some ways in which they can be attended to.

The Power of Poetry for School Leadership provides leaders with a three-part framework: Decision making, problem solving, and communicating grounded in the growing body of literature on organizational behavior and development, and the literature on spirituality in the workplace that can apply to the school setting. This book is not presented as a panacea or an attempt to answer with poetry all the problems of schools. The aim is not to prescribe, but rather to enrich leadership thinking by presenting some information and ideas that cast light on how school leaders may deal with complexities and challenges within today's school environment.

Increasingly, over the past decade, scholars have been calling attention to the spiritual elements of work. *The Stirring of the Soul in the Workplace* (Briskin, 1996); *Leading with Soul: An Uncommon Journey of Spirit* (Bolman and Deal, 1995); *Moral Leadership: Getting to the Heart of School Improvement* (Sergiovanni, 1992); *Spirited Leading and Learning* (Vail, 1998); *Encouraging the Heart* (Kouzes and Posner, 1999) are among recent works dealing with that aspect of our humanity that remains the same through the centuries. *The Power of Poetry for School Leadership* is intended to further the discussion of leadership for the 21st century.

INTENDED AUDIENCE

This book has been written for leaders who want to continually explore new ways of dealing with the challenges inherent in leadership today. It is intended for leaders who want to serve their organizations by increasing their ability to be attentive to the needs of their followers, insightful in interpreting the environment, and effective in their communication. Hence, it is meant not only for principals but for a much broader range of educational professionals, including superintendents, teachers, and leaders outside the field of education.

It could be said that poets serve society primarily by their attention to detail, their insights into life, and their contribution to the human spirit. In destitute times the role of the poet becomes even more critical, since people are likely to move from crisis to crisis without time for reflection. Inspired by the line: "What are poets for in a destitute time?" from German poet Friedrich Hölderlin's poem, "Bread and Wine" (Watts, 1993), this book examines the role poets play in society and the context in which public education exists, and it establishes a link between poetry and school leadership.

The assumptions or theories behind this book are primarily the human resource theories that emphasize the interdependence between people and organizations, and the symbolic theories that focus on problems of meaning, particularly the need to create meaning in organizations. Additionally, the new science of complexity theory is used to help frame the context of schools.

Combining the craft and artistry of poetry with the needs of people in organizations, I have attempted to delineate ways in which school leaders can use aspects of the poet's craft to enhance their ability to read and interpret their environment, develop insights, sharpen their communications, and help meet some of the needs within their schools in ways that can help them maneuver the rapids of educational change.

NEED FOR THE BOOK

Schools are about people, relationships, and learning. In spite of the separation of church and state and the tendency to attribute things spiritual to the church and things intellectual to the state, the people in schools do not or should not be asked to lead dichotomous lives. For the most part, we have shied away from publicly acknowledging the importance of human spirituality. However, one does not put one's humanity on hold when one enters the workplace. That the realities of human existence do not necessarily fit the traditional mode of thinking about people and organizations or fit with popular culture is no excuse for silence. Our reluctance "to recognize spirit as a fundamental life force and source of human energy in our theorizing and research" (Rodriguez, 2001, 23) on schools may very well contribute to some of the challenges of building community in schools.

Poets usually address matters of the heart, the spirit, the soul, those aspects of life often kept hidden in the world of work. N. W. Walter (1962) posits that the poet's mission is to find out what is going on and interpret it to those who see but do not understand. He further notes that poets have a willingness to face the problems of life and try to interpret them, as well as the desire to discover the significance of common things. If ever there were a need to discover the significance of common things—things as common as the human need for meaning—it is today.

Traditionally, in the world of work, people in organizations tend to be more technical, procedural, and scientific and less creative, imaginative, passionate, or spiritual. And today the new economy dictates speed and continuous innovation that are likely to give rise to more formulas with which to manage the explosion of information. Yet, as E. E. Lawler (2001) points out, the era of human capital has arrived—an era in which people are valued for their ability to think, analyze, and problem solve. As people are called on to apply more personal skill in the workplace, their need for meaning in work life becomes paramount. Perhaps the poet's craft, with its mission to search the environment and interpret it, to face the problems of life and try to interpret them, and particularly to discover the significance in common things, can be useful here.

Schools are in need of effective and excellent leadership today more than ever. There are new expectations of and demands on school leaders due in large measure to the changing social, economic, demographic, and structural context in which schools operate. Changing performance expectations and ever-increasing demands for accountability are forcing school districts to seek new kinds of leaders.

The primary goal of this book is to help in the development of the kind of leaders who can pay closer attention to the needs of people in schools.

The Power of Poetry for School Leadership can provide a new lens on familiar activity by offering a different perspective from which to examine and address challenges facing schools. I trust that some of the ideas can become powerful tools for change by suggesting new ways in which events and situations can be perceived.

This book is not meant to be a guide or template for the moves leaders should make, but rather a tool for helping leaders to think deeply about their practices and the needs of those in their charge.

SCOPE OF THE BOOK

Part 1 discusses the context in which school leaders operate. Although much of what has been articulated in part 1 has been said elsewhere and may not be unfamiliar to the reader, it is important as a frame of reference on which to build the argument for the potential uses of poetry in the complex life of public schooling. Just as the context of a poem is critical to its understanding, similarly, the context of schooling is critical to understanding how and even why the process of poetry—poetic thinking and writing—could potentially be useful in finding new ways to deal with the complexities and challenges of school life. The impact of the external context is followed by a discussion of the internal context and the nature of school leadership. Complexity theory is used to frame some aspects of the school environment.

Part 2 is centered on the value of poetry. Poetry is defined; its value, its devices, and its uses are discussed. This is followed by poetry as communication and as a soul-making activity, which sets the stage for introducing the usefulness of techniques of poetry in school leadership.

Part 3 of the book focuses on how leaders can communicate for information and inspiration by using aspects of poetry in their leadership activities. The concept of perceptive practice and a model of perceptive leadership is introduced. The rest of this section focuses on managing and interpreting information from the external context, inspiring those within the organization, and enhancing the leader's communication in light of the devices of poetry.

Acknowledgments

Thanks to a faithful friend and scholar, Christine Emmons, who willingly provided insightful feedback and edited the manuscript. I must acknowledge and extend thanks to David Pettigrew, a colleague who introduced me to Holderlin's work and at whose on-campus conference I presented my earliest articulation of the linkage between poetry and school leadership. Thanks is also extended to two of my colleagues, Christine Broadbridge, who gave encouraging comments on my first foray into this topic at a local conference, and Christine Villani, who, on a whim, suggested I write a book. Student assistants Shelly, Sherry Ann, and Crystal, who persistently made trips to the library and typed, deserve credit. And most important, to my daughter, Renelle K. Richardson, who not only believed that I could and should write this book, but cooked and sometimes cleaned so that I could. Thanks a million to all of you.

Part 1

CHALLENGES
OF SCHOOL LEADERSHIP

Part 1 examines the contexts in which school leaders operate. The discussion centers on the influence of the external environment, the challenges of the internal context, and the complexity they present to school leaders.

Chapter One

The External Context

Why would anyone think we are living in destitute times? Complex, yes. Difficult, yes. Challenging, yes. Perhaps *destitute* is too strong a word, but I was certainly intrigued by the line "What are poets for in a destitute time?" from Friedrich Hölderlin's poem "Bread and Wine."

For public schools, destitution is embodied in the constellation of interrelated and ongoing social, economic, political, and technological changes that lead to continuously new expectations and the challenges this poses for schools and the people working within them.

That schools do not operate in isolation is an overstatement of the obvious. The environment in which schools operate is of such complex nature that one could not discuss schools or school leadership without reference to the impact of the external context. Currently, there are new expectations of, and demands on, school leaders due in large measure to the changing social, demographic, economic, and technological context in which they operate.

Changing performance expectations and ever-increasing demands for accountability are forcing school districts to seek new kinds of leaders. This new kind of leader must be adept at, among other things, scanning the external environment for what is of significance to schools, understanding the internal environment, and communicating in ways that create meaning for their various audiences.

The policy climate is demanding. National, state, and local policy makers advocate new programs and curriculums, demand results, and scrutinize endless amounts of data to see whether schools are performing acceptably. Public schools serve a vital role in the economic development of both the nation and their local communities. This vital economic purpose of schooling puts it at the center of the myriad changes occurring in our world, which makes it an increasingly complex process. The new kind of leader must understand this complex nature of schools and how schools need to relate to the external environment.

One aspect of the science of complexity—the study of complex adaptive systems—may be useful in understanding intricate organizational dynamics. As defined by Lewin and Regine (2000), complex adaptive systems are composed of diverse agents that interact with each other, mutually affect each other, and in so doing, generate novel behavior for the system as a whole.

Schools are situated in a rapidly and constantly changing environment, and when the environment changes, so, too, does the behavior of those within schools—though the change within schools is hardly ever a replication of the magnitude of the change in the environment. As we are well aware, over time, schools have been undergoing ceaseless restructuring, reform, or adaptation to the demands placed on them.

So complexity theory may be useful in understanding schools in relation to their environment, because schools can be considered complex adaptive systems. This means that what complexity scientists are learning about natural systems may have the potential to illuminate some aspects of schooling. Let's briefly examine some factors in the external environment that significantly impact life within schools and pose challenges for school leaders.

ONGOING SOCIAL CHANGES

Societal forces impact schools continually. Since the inception of public schools, there has been a direct link between the national social agenda and the curriculum in schools. A quick review of some key events in the history of public education shows that, from the 1874 Supreme Court ruling that gave states the right to levy taxes to support public schools up to the 2002 Bush Education Plan, public schools have been called upon to meet the needs—economic, defense, and otherwise—of this democracy.

A growing child psychology movement gave rise to progressive education between World War I and World War II and an associated attempt to educate all students. With the Soviet Sputnik flight in 1957, progressive education became a target for criticism. Americans were concerned that the United States was losing the space race to the Soviets. Federal money was therefore spent on math, science, history, and foreign languages, with the focus on academically talented students. Next came federal legislation that supported training and programs in subject areas deemed vital to defense. The National Defense Act of 1958 singled out science, math, modern languages, and guidance as the major focus of education, and money was supplied for curriculum development in those areas.

The 1960s and early 1970s ushered in a period during which the social conscience came to the fore, coinciding with concerns for poverty, racial discrimination, and equal opportunity. The focus shifted to disadvantaged students, and Title I, the Elementary and Secondary Education Act of 1965, provided compensatory funding.

By the mid-1970s the definition of *disadvantaged* was enlarged to include multicultural, bilingual, handicapped, and women, and federal funds were made available for bilingual and special education. The mid-1980s saw national attention turn to excellence and higher academic standards, driven by several reports on the dismal performance of American students when compared with other countries. This ushered in two waves of school reform, the era of accountability and the standards movement.

It is quite evident that schools have repeatedly been called upon to carry the burden of patriotism and national defense. Whether it was competing with the Soviets in the space race, saving the nation from Communism and later from Japanese economic competition, or being first in the world, public schooling has been adapting to changes in the environment since its inception, and these social changes and tensions engender changes in the role of school leaders.

Take, for example, the role of the school superintendent, which has changed significantly over time. Social changes in the 1960s and 1970s, reform in the 1980s and 1990s, the growth in state and federal mandates, and the accountability movement have all impacted school leadership at the district level in terms of authority and policy making. In the 1990s, the choice movement and advocacy for more control at the local level by principals, parents, teachers, and students have brought additional challenges to the superintendents' authority and policy-making leadership.

When one understands the purpose of public schooling, it becomes increasingly clear that those who choose positions of school leadership must have at their disposal a wide array of skills to deal with the multiplicity of issues they encounter within and outside of schools. Changes similar to those at the district level impact school leaders at the building level, where they encounter additional challenges of immediate concern to their students, teachers, and communities.

DEMOGRAPHIC IMPACT

Ongoing and predictable demographic changes also contribute to the complex environment in which schools operate. Since school districts are fiscally dependent on their local communities, demographic shifts are likely to have a major financial impact on public schools. The question looms as to whether the aging baby boomers (an estimated seventy million people) will maintain their interest and support of public schools after their children have graduated. This could exacerbate the politics of public schooling, particularly in the area of local funding.

Furthermore, the changing demographic makeup of many school districts, in which as many as twenty or more languages coexist, highlights the need for an increase in not only the number of foreign-language teachers, at a time when teachers are in short supply, but also in the number of teachers who are able to understand the needs of culturally diverse students. Increased global travel and immigration continue to alter the demographic makeup of classrooms. Moreover, the recent inclusion of special-needs students presents its own set of challenges to which schools must adjust.

ECONOMIC CHANGES

Recent indicators of the extravagance in everyday American life appear to confirm the egregious disparities in wealth that can pose challenges to schools. During the late 1990s to early 2000s, in an age of prosperity, in which a nineteen-year-old with an idea for a software company was able to in a few years accumulate a net worth that exceeds the gross national product of some Third World countries, poverty among children was still rising in several parts of this country. The juxtaposition of wealth and need is striking.

Take, for example, the state of Connecticut, one of the smallest and wealthiest states in the union. A recent report shows that the state's child poverty rate increased from 11 percent in 1989 to 15 percent in 1997, resulting in about 40,000 more children (approximately 120,000 total) living in poverty (Geballe and Hall, 2001). While the issue is one of relative poverty, the magnitude of differences in income and wealth is staggering, and these differences account for inequities in educational funding among school districts.

The transformation of the economic system has exerted significant impact on schools as economic changes have reshaped American values. Increased wealth has accelerated the pace of change in values and, subsequently, moral concerns. The relationship between capitalism and social decay is becoming increasingly clear, as businesses, in their drive to increase profit, engage in unethical practices. The recent high-profile corporate debacles such as Enron and WorldCom exemplify this phenomenon in no small measure. Others, in their drive for success, cater, through advertising and media productions, to some of the more harmful elements of the culture.

Since there is an integral link between schools and society, with social demands filtering down to the schools, the social consequences of the new economy pose increasing challenges to schools. Moreover, as trends in society create the impetus for schools to continually restructure and add to the already overburdened curriculum, schools are likely to become overwhelmed.

The recent prevalence of programs in character education is one such example. In some wealthy communities, students require specialized psychological assistance to deal with the problem of having everything material they desire and are trying to find meaning and purpose in life. At the same time, other students need continuous social-work interventions to help them cope with the host of problems associated with poverty.

TECHNOLOGICAL ADVANCES

There is also the question of the social and moral costs to be paid for the benefits of advances in areas like biotechnology, which holds myriad ethical issues. High school biology classrooms are being transformed, as students grapple with issues such as the use of gene therapy, aimed at curing diseases, as well as gene enhancement, aimed at improving human beings. Furthermore, in the new field of artificial life, scientists are experimenting with the creation of human life by using silicon to replicate human thought, mobility, expression, and reproduction. These are issues of ethics, values, and morality, which schools must be prepared to address.

Instructional technology has the potential to fundamentally change not only the notion of school, but also the organization of school leadership. Maurer and Davidson (1998) see the use of technology to support an effective and quality academic program as a revolutionary, systemic change that alters a school's culture. Technology, they say, causes learners to do things differently, causes teachers to change their methods and strategies, and causes the school community to adapt its shared goals and its values and beliefs about teaching and learning to accommodate a new culture. The traditional leadership function, based on formal leaders and followers who exist in an environment of differential power, is inconsistent with this requisite change in the school's culture.

But technology is doing more than changing instruction. The Internet poses challenges for schools, primarily in terms of usage, censorship, and exposure to previously less-accessible materials, such as pornography, to students in K–12 settings.

Advances in technology have played a major role in both highlighting the nature of our destitution and exacerbating the chasm between the wealthy and the poor. There are the digital haves and the digital have-nots. While some students are already well connected into the global network of information and opportunity, others lead a technologically deprived existence. The mass affluence created in the United States leaves many school districts grappling with the challenges inherent in both poverty and prosperity simultaneously.

NEW EXPECTATIONS FOR SCHOOLS

At the same time that schools are struggling to respond to the impact of poverty and prosperity and the impact of technology, they are subjected to increased public scrutiny. Largely driven by international comparisons of American students on standardized tests, *accountability* has become the watchword of a skeptical public. Contemporary school leaders are required to spend more time with community groups, to be highly visible, and to deal with increasing public criticism and demands.

During the past decade, the pressure for educational reform has increased and school leaders have been faced with the need to act decisively to improve schools. Recently, national and state standards have been established and standardized testing has increased. Teachers and school leaders are, for the most part, left to make sense of the standards and to ensure that test scores are high. Additionally, part of the present-day context of school leadership is the pivotal role of the leader as key to implementing various school change efforts.

In enumerating the tasks of educational leaders, the National Council for Accreditation of Teacher Education (NCATE) (National Policy Board, 1995), the accrediting organization for schools, colleges, and departments of education in the United States, describes the role as requiring patience and perspective, the exercise of judgment and wisdom, the development of new technical and analytical skills, sensitivities to other cultures, highly developed communication skills, and personal values that integrate the ethical dimensions of decision making. The Interstate School Leaders Licensure Consortium (ISLLC) published six standards through which educational leaders should promote the success of all students.

Leadership assessments proliferate among the various professional organizations and state departments of education. Standards have been published by organizations such as the National Policy Board for Educational Administration (NPBEA), the National Association of Secondary School Principals (NASSP), and the American Association of School Administrators (AASA), all proposing similar new expectations for school leaders. Together these standards and others that are emerging for school leaders attempt to delineate what is to be done in the turbulence of school life.

CHALLENGES TO LEADERS

Since public education is integrally linked with federal, state, and local governments; businesses; community groups; and social service agencies, schools cannot be divorced from politics. Consequently, school leaders operate in a highly politicized environment. At the same time they're dealing with internal politics, they are facing mounting external obligations as the demands on public schools increase.

As can be seen, the complexity of the position has increased, and today, school leadership is among the most challenging leadership positions. The external environment poses several challenges to those who lead schools and school districts.

The Task Force on School District Leadership (2001) sums up the changing priorities in this manner:

> District leaders are operating in an environment of ever-shifting priorities. During the first half of the twentieth century, says the conventional wisdom, district management could be defined by "the four B's": Bonds, Budgets, Buses and Buildings. By the 1970s, it had become "the four R's—Race, Resources, Relationships and Rules—as heretofore mostly ignored groups such as members of minority groups, teachers, students, and communities began asserting themselves. Priorities shifted again in the 1980s when the contemporary school reform movement gained traction. Today, district leaders must concern themselves with a host of different concerns: "the four A's": Academic standards, Accountability, Autonomy and Ambiguity and "the five C's": Collaboration, Communication, Connection, Child advocacy and Community building. (2)

As R. E. Lane (2002) sees it, the human spirit is made dull by powerful economic and political systems that assure material comfort but seem unable to bring deeper meaning or lasting happiness to our lives. Upon examination, the five C's appear to focus much more intently than previous priorities on issues dealing with the human spirit and meaning. Public school administrators today are being asked to build bridges, re-create community, and provide meaning—a tall order for any leader.

The responsibilities and problems inherent in the positions of school leadership are wide in scope and variety. As advocates for children, schools play an essential role in the life of the local community. As the social, behavioral, and academic needs of students change, new kinds of links between schools and the external community are required. School leaders are more challenged than ever before to maintain constant contact with a bewildering array of internal and external stakeholders, to share information, and to request feedback on a wide range of issues relating to the education of young people.

It is quite clear that school leaders, whether at the district or building level, need to be expert problem analyzers and problem solvers as well as human relations experts. This skill set requires the ability to organize large amounts of information, to see the big picture, to store and retrieve information quickly, and get to the salient aspect of situations. The need has become much more urgent today as boundaries between schools and their environments dissolve.

Recent reform efforts call for principals and superintendents to engage in collaborative leadership. For many, this may require additional time, effort, and the development of abilities to engage with the community to a greater degree than they currently do.

Because of the changing nature of the environment and the high degree of uncertainty, school leaders must pay increased attention to external environments and build strong relationships with their stakeholders. As boundary spanners, school leaders play a major role in filtering information between the organization and the environment.

Elements in the environment are changing constantly, and these changes impact schools. Leaders must develop the ability to understand how environmental change will impact the school and must develop the ability to respond to these environmental changes. This type of activity requires tremendous insight on the part of the school leader, who must constantly make decisions regarding the strategic position of the school or district relative to its environment.

School leaders do not have it within their power to reduce the dependencies between schools and their environment, or to change the environment. In order to devise effective adaptive strategies to increase collaboration between the school and the environment, they must develop a penchant for scanning their environment. Attempting collaboration in an open system, such as a school, poses its own set of decision-making challenges. This open-systems view of organizations emphasizes the interrelationships between the organization and its environment. An important aspect of the open-systems model is the organization's adaptation to the changing environment.

School leaders need to become highly analytical in reading and interpreting the environment, as well as masterful in communicating the information to those within the organization, in ways that cultivate purpose and meaning. Equally important is the ability to communicate effectively with their various audiences and stakeholders.

As the Task Force on School District Leadership (2001) points out, school leaders must be comfortable with managing media relations, public meetings, and politically inspired pressures, and they must be adept at developing both permanent and temporary coalitions with often disparate community groups. While the challenges in dealing with the external environment appear formidable, those in the internal school environment appear to be no less so.

Chapter Two

The Internal Context

In examining the internal context, the issue of boundaries between schools and their communities warrants further attention. Boundary spanning is becoming an increasingly important role of school leaders. As schools become responsible for functions previously within the purview of the home, religious organizations, or social service agencies, boundaries become blurred and leaders are required to expand their reach in information gathering, decision making, problem solving, and communication. Although boundary spanning is carried out by many people in the school district simultaneously, it is important to focus on the boundary spanning of leaders.

In reality, school leaders make few choices on their own. Whether involved primarily with stakeholders outside of or within the school, leaders are involved in a dance of sorts as they try to make sense of the confluence of interests that impact their decision making. Collecting information by constantly scanning their environments is essential to decision making.

Balancing the tensions of dependence on the external environment with the challenges in the internal environment is perhaps one of the most underrated aspects of school leadership. While various pressures are brought to bear on the schools, life within the school poses its own set of complexities. There are no clear-cut boundaries between schools' internal and external environments; however, there is definitely a different set of internal issues with which leaders must contend.

The internal context of school is no less daunting than the external. Along with the usual expectations for higher academic standards, schools currently face a long list of expectations and needs generated by families and by society. Among them are before- and after-school child care, health services, and psychological support. In addition, myriad needs surface from staff, faculty, students, and the district.

Schools have been variously described as fast-paced, fragmented, and unpredictable environments with a need for quick decision making, continuous problem solving, fast storage and retrieval of information, and ongoing communication. This unique culture of schools challenges the leader's cognitive abilities, emotional and psychological strength, ethical values, as well as physical stamina.

THE UNIQUE CULTURE OF SCHOOLS

Schools, it is commonly said, have a culture all their own. Noting a decades-old observation that is still relevant today, Deal and Peterson (1999) cite Willard Waller's (1932) observation that schools have a culture that is definitely their own with complex rituals of personal relationships, folkways, mores, irrational sanctions, games, wars, teams, and an elaborate set of ceremonies concerning them, as well as traditions, and traditionalists waging their old-world battle against innovators. Several scholars concur with a definition of culture as a system of shared values and beliefs that interact with an organization's people, organizational structures, and control systems to produce behavioral norms. In practical terms, this definition helps make clear that *shared values* means what is important; *beliefs* means what we think is true; and *behavioral norms* means how we do things around here (Owens, 2001).

However defined, culture is seen as a profound force that shapes people's behavior, perception, and understanding of events in their environment and consequently impacts how the organization responds to change in its environment. For schools, dependent as they are on the environment, the development of a culture that sustains them is critical. This powerful, intangible force, school culture, is created by the people in schools and at the same time influences their behavior. It does not take long for new teachers to be advised about how things really work in a school, and consequently how they should behave. Although decisions are not made independently, school leaders can greatly influence the culture of a school.

People seek order, stability, and meaning in their work and find ways to create that for themselves. Hence, unwritten expectations, traditions, and rules develop over time. It is conceivable that an organization's culture can stifle innovation and hard work, or conversely, it can engender commitment and creativity. It is incumbent on leaders to take deliberate steps to help shape the culture through their actions and their communication.

The influence and importance of culture are summed up by Deal and Peterson (1999) in this manner: "This deeper structure of life in organizations is reflected and transmitted through symbolic language and expressive action. Culture consists of the stable, underlying social meanings that shape beliefs and behavior over time" (7). What culture seems to describe without necessarily naming it so, are deeper issues at the core of the human experience—issues of faith, hope, love, a search for meaning, for happiness, and fulfillment. At the core of this deeper structure in organizational life rests the needs of the human heart.

THE IMPORTANCE OF HUMAN NEEDS

As I see it, the interplay of people, programs, and practices converges to determine the culture within schools. The leader's behavior in relation to these three factors is a critical influence on the development of the culture of the school.

Essentially, schools are made up of people. Hence, it would be vitally important to examine the human underpinnings of the organization. However, when one considers the organization from the popularly used scientific management perspective, the things that one can measure, quantify, and control, such as organizational structure, rules and regulations, policy decisions, and programs, seem to be given more attention and reinforcement than those things that cannot be easily measured, quantified, or controlled.

In this view, the human side of organization seems less important. Values, beliefs, culture, behavioral norms, and the like are considered nice to take into consideration, if one even gets the programs under way. Yet, these are the aspects of schooling that may be more powerful in getting things done, because they concern critical human needs. Leaders are challenged to orchestrate some balance between the measurable, quantifiable, and controllable elements and the relational, emotional, and social aspects of schooling.

Bolman and Deal (1991) provide a valuable lens through which to examine people in organizations. Their human resource frame starts from the premise that people's skills, insights, ideas, energy, and commitment are an organization's most critical resource. Applying this frame to schools in no way indicates that programs are not important; rather it serves to highlight the importance of people and their needs.

But, in this age of unending school reform, there has been an overemphasis on picking the right programs, and it is not uncommon to hear teachers complain of having had to change programs too often, or conversely, to hear administrators boast about the various programs present in their schools. Generally, the programs are first selected or mandated and then the people are called upon to adjust and readjust to them. The modus operandi is programs first, people second. This practice could, in large measure, account for much of the resistance that is common in schools. When the emphasis shifts to people first, the energy spent on establishing practices that meet the needs of the people responsible for implementing the programs might result in less resistance.

Bolman and Deal's (1991) human resource frame draws on a body of research and theory built around assumptions that speak directly to human needs:

1. Organizations exist to serve human needs (rather than the reverse).
2. Organizations and people need each other. (Organizations need ideas, energy, and talent; people need careers, salaries, and work opportunities.)
3. When the fit between the individual and the organization is poor, one or both will suffer: individuals will be exploited, or will seek to exploit the organizations, or both.
4. A good fit between individual and organization benefits both: human beings find meaningful and satisfying work, and organizations get the human talent and energy that they need. (121)

The first two assumptions are particularly useful to keep in mind as we examine issues in the internal context of schooling. While there exists a multiplicity of dissimilar needs demonstrated by people in any school, the needs of the human heart are, if not the same, quite similar. Schools are places of learning, not only for students but for everyone in the school.

Consequently, it is prevailing practice to share knowledge. At the risk of sounding like a cliché, "people don't care how much you know until they know how much you care." So caring is as critical as sharing knowledge.

When caring does not emanate from the practices within a school, when people's needs are not being met, they tend not to care and to resist more vociferously. For example, *how* a leader goes about asking or telling staff to implement a change makes a tremendous difference in what, if anything, ever gets implemented. When people are asked to make a change and they perceive that their needs, whether for information, support, or encouragement, are not met, they are less likely to comply.

One can easily take issue with the concept of need or what people need from their experiences within organizations, because needs are hard to define and difficult to measure. In education today, measurement or assessment is a major driving force in reform. Since the needs of the human heart are not easily measured, it is easier to focus solely on what is measurable and quantifiable, which runs counter to the ability of leaders to build strong collaborative relationships.

The idea that people have needs is a central element in psychology. Maslow (1954) categorizes human needs into a hierarchy from "lower" to "higher," with lower psychological, safety, and belonging needs dominating behavior when they are not satisfied, and higher needs, such as self-esteem and self-actualization, becoming salient only *after* the lower needs have been satisfied. In schools, today, because of recent waves of violence, safety has become a more prevalent and explicit need. The needs for belonging and love are also important, and when they predominate, a leader's focus should be different from that required when self-actualization is the dominant need.

The concept of need in schools, then, is important to the leader, who should accept responsibility to cultivate conditions in the environment that allow people to thrive and be productive. The leader must be acutely aware of the high level of interdependence between the schools and the people who work in them. The needs people seek to satisfy in organizations range from economic to personal and social. Schools in turn cannot function effectively without the energy and talent of their employees. To produce a win/win situation, both the needs of the individual and the needs of the organization must be attended to.

This role of producing harmony between the needs of the school and those of individuals should not be taken lightly, since it has serious consequences for both the individual and the organization. When their needs are not being met, individuals feel disconnected, apathetic, or exploited, and this invariably negatively affects performance. On the deeper level, the human spirit is affected, and people do not feel comfortable sharing from their hearts or baring their souls at work. In this way the workplace has the potential to cause spiritual harm. Consequently, school leaders must be attentive to the practices, behaviors, and values within a school because they impact individual lives.

UNDERSTANDING THE COMPLEX
NATURE OF THE INTERNAL ENVIRONMENT

Schools and school leaders are in the challenging and complex situation of having to continuously respond to the environment while cultivating the culture within the school.

Several aspects of a complex adaptive system are descriptive of school environments. That the boundaries are fuzzy and agents and the system are adaptive; that systems are embedded within other systems and co-evolve; and that tension and paradox are natural phenomena, not necessarily to be resolved, could not be truer of any organization than they are of schools.

Plsek and Greenhalgh (2001) describe complex adaptive systems as a collection of individual agents with freedom to act in ways that are not always totally predictable, and whose actions are interconnected so that one agent's actions change the context for other agents. An agent's actions are based on internalized rules that need not be shared, explicit, or even logical when viewed by another. Additionally, complex systems have fuzzy rather than rigid boundaries.

The science of complex adaptive systems may provide an important perspective from which to examine some of the challenges of schooling, particularly issues relating to human needs within organizations. The new theory emanating from complexity science not only puts people and relationships at the center of things, but also casts light on the significance and the attention that should be placed on how people interact with each other and the kinds of relationships they form. Human beings are anything but binary. They are infinitely complex. School people operate in a nonlinear, dynamic world, where everything exists only in relationship to everything else. The structure and purpose of schooling, coupled with human needs, present a unique array of complex issues for the school leader.

One underrated aspect of working in schools is the fact that everyone has had some experience with learning. This learning occurred, most likely, in a school or at home. The point is that adults bring their past experiences of schooling with them, and this can influence how they deal with issues within the school. In examining the deeper nature of schooling, it is important to keep this unique aspect of the organization in mind. Countless philosophical perspectives coexist and add to the complex nature of the internal school environment.

With the increasing complexity and ambiguity of schooling and the ensuing challenge of culture building, school leaders must find ways to understand and work with the deep nature of schooling. That schools seem to be existing in this nonlinear dynamic world where interactions lead to unpredictable outcomes appears obvious. What is not as obvious is the most effective ways in which the leader can help those they lead make sense and find deeper meaning in their work. Where, then, should the leader focus?

School leaders cannot control their organizations to the degree that scientific management implies. They can, however, influence where their school is heading and how it evolves, primarily through establishing mission, vision, values, and goals. But this cannot be done in isolation or by looking only to what is happening in the external environment. In order to influence where their schools are going or how they can evolve, it would be important for school leaders to carefully examine the nature of the relationships within the school.

WHAT MATTERS MOST

There is an emerging emphasis on relationships within schools. On a practical level, Geertz's (1973) description of culture as the web of significance in which we all are suspended casts some light on the importance of relationships. The leader has to have some skill in engendering significance among the people in an organization, but that web cannot be woven by the leader alone. The leader may display the blueprint and enroll others to join in the weaving. The leader may head up the design team for the blueprint, or may commission the blueprint to a group. If the leader's task is to ensure that significance is built in for all people in the organization, it would be important to seek out the diverse perspectives that exist within the organization. For the leader, this means focusing attention on what matters most.

What matters most is the meaning that people derive from the activities in which they engage. This requires that school leaders focus attention on the informal, the symbolic, and the subtle aspects of school life. The interrelationships among the people, the programs, and the practices provide opportunities for focusing on issues of significance. School leaders must engage those who work in schools to develop a mission and a vision and introduce values and goals to help people establish practices that will enable the various programs to be effective.

In the process of building the mission and vision and clarifying values and establishing goals, teachers, parents, and students respond to some basic questions that give insights into what is meaningful to them. These include questions such as: Why do we exist? What is important here? Why do we function the way we do? What do we hope to become? What do we believe in? How must we behave in order to realize our vision?

In answering such questions they are not simply constructing a mission or vision statement, they are articulating ways in which they can experience purpose and meaning. They are articulating what makes them feel significant and what matters most to them. They are giving the leader clues about the conditions that will stir their souls at work.

Helping others feel significant means paying attention to what matters to them, to what is meaningful to them. It is incumbent on the leader to become the person who can effectively orchestrate these dynamics and engender some kind of harmonious relationship among people. In this endeavor a leader must be able to lead from the heart. The ability of a leader to influence the culture of a school emanates directly from who the leader is at the core. Integrity, credibility, and trust are essential, as is the ability to focus on the needs of others.

To influence how a school evolves, school leaders must manage change, and the key factor in change is what it means to those who must implement it. The human need for meaning is paramount in times of change. And, since schools exist in a state of perpetual change, it is critical that school leaders examine, understand, and define their meaning-making role. Marris (1975) explains that change provokes loss, challenges competence, creates confusion, and causes conflict. The leader in this type of environment is challenged primarily to help others make meaning and maintain a sense of purpose.

This tension between seeing change as loss versus seeing change as renewal has enormous implications for the enterprise of school reform, and for the prime responsibility of school leaders in managing change and all its ramifications. In order to implement new programs, people are called upon to change their practices with unprecedented frequency.

And so, school leaders must understand the mixed feelings and anxiety that accompany any change. Addressing these feelings in themselves and in those they lead is vital for leaders to successfully implement change. The leader is responsible for helping those they lead make connections between the old and the new, find patterns and meaning, and feel significant throughout the change effort. The nature of this type of leadership requires a much more humane model for leading than scientific management has given us.

As we grapple with moving away from scientific management to the more humane method of leadership for schools, Hoyle (2002) takes the discourse into a new realm by addressing the concept of love as the key to effective leadership. He points out that in spite of the millions spent on preparing executives to lead organizations, love-based interpersonal communication, the most important skill other than business ethics, is stressed little, if at all. The emerging reconceptualization of school leadership as moral, caring, loving, and spiritual poses its own set of challenges to leaders socialized in an era of leadership understood as command and control.

Chapter Three

The Nature of School Leadership

As I see it, there is a place for command and control in leadership. That place is squarely on leaders themselves. Leaders are responsible for themselves as much as for those they lead. The notion of command and control then should shift from others to self. This means instead of attempting to command and control others, a leader commands, controls, or wills the self to do what is necessary in light of the changing needs of the organization. This is a critically important issue, since it is just as easy for leaders to get used to their comfort zones and resist change as it is for their followers. Hence, self-leadership precedes leading others.

Leaders must be acutely aware of their own attitudes and dispositions as they go about the tasks of leading. Human organizations have been variously described; however, Bolman and Deal (1991), in describing them as places that can be snake pits as well as rose gardens, draw attention to both the challenge of leading a human organization and the critically important role leaders of such organizations play.

The snake pit metaphor is diametrically opposed to the rose garden metaphor, which conjures up images of a place of beauty, where love abounds, where the heart sings, and where the soul and spirit thrive. The leader plays a pivotal role in helping to shape the kind of metaphor that would describe a school as it evolves.

Taken together, heart, spirit, soul, and love are all themes that dominate the poet's craft. If anyone can speak simultaneously to these aspects of our human existence, it is the poet. If these, then, are surfacing as explicit needs within schools that should be addressed by leaders, how should they lead? In part 3 of this book, I attempt to indulge school leaders in the realm of poetry to provide some answers to this question. Let us, however, first look more closely at the role of the school leader.

Against the backdrop of a complex and ambiguous external context and a challenging internal context with blurred boundaries, school leaders must be adept at managing complexity, building community, and touching the hearts, souls, and spirits of those within schools.

MANAGING COMPLEXITY

A closer look at the complexity of schooling shows the leader grappling with elements in the external environment, while simultaneously working to clarify purpose and create meaning within the school. This has given rise to new metaphors for school leadership. Wheatley (1999), for example, describes the leader's work as a dance rather than a forced march. Donaldson (2001) concludes that the talents school leaders need are those more befitting a choreographer, who, as a leader, also participates as a dancer in an ongoing recital of working relationships, purposes, and teaching and learning action. "As they whirl around the floor, their goals are to build relationships, clarify purposes, and facilitate action-in-common so that all people train their energies and talents on learning. . . . They thus enliven the three streams of leadership, energizing the dancers to step more energetically, more fluidly, and more in harmony with one another" (107–108). This vivid metaphor of school leader as choreographer alludes to harmony, happiness, and a sense of significance.

There is no question that the day-to-day life of the typical school leader is fraught with problems to be solved. In order to execute their roles well, school leaders are called primarily to be expert problem analyzers and problem solvers. How then do they choreograph the people, programs, and practices into this harmonious dance of significance? Or, have they even thought it possible to find harmony and engender significance in such a problem-laden situation?

My present metaphor of school leader as poet addresses this need for high levels of analysis. It speaks to the qualities of the mood and spirit of poetry that can positively enhance leadership with deeper insight and greater attention and to some of the technical qualities of poetry that can enhance leaders' communication. Poets hone their craft by analyzing the totality of the human experience, its pleasures as well as its problems, the noble as well as the ignoble.

Public schools are undergoing rapid transformation and require high levels of analytical and relational skills in managing the fast-paced and unpredictable environment. In a typical day, filled with the need to make quick decisions, school leaders fill multidimensional roles wherein they need to be expert problem analyzers and problem framers, collecting and interpreting information, perceiving what is of significance, planning for solutions, and making meaning, as well as focusing on issues of direct concern with students and the school's mission, vision, values, and goals. Rather than looking just at the unique circumstances surrounding each decision, leaders must see the big picture. They must master information storage and retrieval in order to analyze and solve problems. The ability to survey the changing environment, grasp the big picture, identify patterns, and communicate with teachers and students in ways that nurture relationships, build community, make sense, and create meaning is paramount.

A study of poetry reveals keen observation, deep analysis, and strong impactful communication as inherent aspects of the craft. These qualities of poetry appear to be quite useful as tools for maneuvering the type of environment in which school leaders function.

Complexity pervades the life of school leaders. In DuFour's (1998) observation of the paradoxical nature of school-level leadership, he notes:

> Principals have been called upon to be strong leaders and to give away power to others, to celebrate the success of their school and to perpetuate discontent with the status quo; to convey urgency regarding the need for school improvement efforts over the long haul; to encourage individual autonomy and to insist on adherence to the school's mission, vision, values, and goals; to build widespread support for change and to push forward with improvement despite resistance; to approach improvement incrementally and to promote the aggressive comprehensive shake-up necessary to escape the bonds of traditional school cultures. (43)

The paradoxes inherent in the internal context of school leadership are inescapable. So, too, are the challenges posed by the external context. This level of complexity can lead to discouragement and frustration. One role of the school leader in dealing with complexity is to assuage the frustration and disillusionment of those they lead as well as their own. At the same time, the school leader must continuously be on the alert to adapt to changes in the complex environment.

As changes accelerate and a new kind of economy and new global threats emerge, leaders are finding many of their underlying assumptions and time-honored ways of working inadequate to help them understand what is going on, let alone how to help others deal with it. School leaders who are still operating under the old scientific management business models, which were predicated on linear thinking, control, and some level of predictability, now find themselves having to function in a much more organic, unpredictable, predominantly nonlinear, boundaryless environment where limited control and a restricted ability to predict are the order of the day. New ways of coping are sought and needed for a new, complex era.

The latest attempt to understand the structure and dynamics of complex systems in the natural world is called complexity theory. Lewin and Regine (2000) draw on the science of complexity to present ideas that create a more human-oriented and successful workplace. They suggest that in today's rapidly changing business environment, a collective effort and a recognized need for others have become the means of survival and success. Interestingly, they believe this change brings with it a new hope and a potential for a deep human resonance within organizations. Because it is predicated on far less control and far less predictability than is assumed in traditional management practice, it simultaneously brings anxiety, uncertainty, and fear.

While there exists a structure within which they function, essentially schools are all about humans, their growth and development. The popular notion "the human side of business" does not readily apply to the school environment. For schools, a totally people business, there is no opposing other side; there is only the human side, making it critically more important that school leaders pay attention to nurturing relationships.

Effective leadership in schools not only entails having "a nose for things," school leaders must also develop "an eye for things" and "a heart for things." The need and ability to gather sense data are quite apparent here. A key in the current environment for school leaders is to focus much more intently on the quality of the relationships and find ways in which they can help create deeper meaning for those who work and learn in the schools.

BUILDING COMMUNITY

Having "an eye for things" and "a heart for things" is at the center of building community, which involves paying attention to relationships, developing shared intentions, and inspiring performance.

We generally think of schools as organizations in which people go to conduct the business of teaching and learning as formal intellectual activities. But, formal organizations require certain kinds of prescribed behaviors that do not usually have to do with the heart, the soul, or the spirit. More exactly, the behaviors we think of in relation to formal organizations refer to visible postures, looks, attitudes, knowledge, and skills. In other words, we focus on the external actions. Internal matters are left unattended or considered not central to the purpose of schooling.

Perhaps we have missed the mark in our characterization of schools as formal organizations. One does not readily conjure up images of a choreographed dance or a rose garden when one thinks of schools. Rather, they are places of hard work, continuous human interactions, and all kinds of interesting memories. Because of the high levels of human interaction in schools, practices that make sense in schools would include those that address matters of the heart, soul, and spirit, in essence, those practices that would facilitate meaning and sense making.

At the dawn of the 21st century, with a new economy and new global concerns, the limitations of classical leadership models are becoming starkly apparent. New ways of thinking about leadership are required, and, judging from the titles of several recent books on leadership, new ideas are emerging. This thinking advocates that school leaders build community, develop shared intentions, inspire performance, in short, attend to the spiritual aspects of being human.

Building community within schools seems to be the clarion call for meeting the human needs as they are emerging within schools. A debate has ensued regarding whether school should be viewed as organization or as community. Sergiovanni (1999) points out that both the organization and the community metaphor ring true for certain aspects of how schools function, but that it makes a world of difference which of the two provides the overarching frame.

While the literature in educational leadership has been pervaded by the belief that schools are formal organizations, and prescriptions for school

leadership have been based on that assumption, a new leadership paradigm has been emerging based on the notion of school as community. In
fact, Sergiovanni calls for changing the metaphor of schooling from organization to community. He writes, "Organization is an idea that is imposed from without. To ensure proper fit, schools create management systems that communicate requirements to teachers in the form of
expectations. Organizations use rules and regulations, monitoring and supervising, and evaluation systems to maintain control over teachers. Leadership in organizations, then, is inevitably control driven" (102). Sergiovanni argues, further, that schools are an inherently moral enterprise and
that moral leadership asks leaders not only to adopt a new mind-set, but
also to act differently.

As previously mentioned, the position taken in this book is that control
does have a place in school leadership. The key is to press the levers of
control in the appropriate place. Rather than directing control over others,
a leader must develop and practice control of the self. Self-control is one
of the keys to acting differently as part of one's moral responsibility.

Several scholars and theorists have heeded Sergiovanni's call to change
the schooling metaphor from organization to community. Maurer and
Davidson (1998), for example, propose the notion of community of leadership. Simply put, the community of leadership comprises the stakeholders in children's education and is facilitated by the formal leader who is
joined and supported by others in the community—an egalitarian model
of leadership that is quite a departure from the traditional conceptualization of leader. It would require a change in the culture of the school environment in which issues of power and control would give way to engaging multiple members of the school community to meet the needs of the
school. This is quite easy to articulate in theory, but extremely messy in
reality.

Giving up or sharing leadership for someone socialized in the power
and control paradigm of leading could constitute a radical change in self-
perception and effectiveness. The dissonance could be discouraging.
Building community involves efforts to create a culture in which people
genuinely care about each other and help each other to lead more productive work lives, thereby increasing the sense of kinship. Although the new
thinking about leadership may represent for many traditional leaders a
role lacking power and influence, even within the new conceptions of col-

laborative school leadership, the principal or formal leader plays a central role. This should not be clouded by the various efforts to build community. The role of the formal leader is vitally important and should in no way be considered replaceable.

In building community, power and influence are possible through the exercise of other skills. Emotional, interpersonal, and intrapersonal skills hold great potential for touching the heart, soul, and spirit, and could help stem the tide of fragmentation caused by classical leadership models that have been imported into schools. Use of these skills by school leaders helps bond people together with a shared set of values and ideas, creating interdependence with and among those they lead. The shared values facilitate decision making that creates meaning and purpose, thereby creating a special sense of belonging.

DEVELOPING SHARED INTENTIONS

Developing shared intentions is a critical function of the school leader who is willing to build a community of learners. This is precisely where mission, vision, values, and goals can be effectively operationalized to provide meaning to people who work in schools. Although to many people in schools, taking the time to develop mission and vision statements appears to be useless, in reality, it is probably one of the best uses of time a leader intent on building a sense of community can engage the staff and faculty in.

Mission and vision statements are totally useless unless they are lived. Answering the question of why we exist, mission addresses fundamental purpose. A desirable future situation is encapsulated in a vision. Values outline priorities and delineate the attitudes, behaviors, and commitments that each group must demonstrate in order to move toward the shared vision. Articulating these aspects of the school is only the starting point of building a community.

The leader's role is to consistently and persistently find ways to enable others to live up to these commitments. A fine distinction here is the leader's ability to capture seemingly simple or mundane issues and make them issues of significance. Through keen observation and use of the imagination, a perceptive leader can see beauty in the commonplace and transform the everyday to new heights. Used in this manner, this set of shared intentions becomes the foundation upon which community is built. It also provides the material for creating symbols and rituals that bind people together.

In spite of all the environmental uncertainty, the needs of the human heart are constant. By appealing to and addressing the needs of the heart, leaders can more readily bring about commitment, than through the use of power and control. This may very well hold a key to effectiveness in today's unpredictable environment.

Appealing to common values as one goes about the day-to-day routines is necessary in helping others keep their commitments. In the process of coordinating, directing, and monitoring school operations; overseeing teaching and learning; engaging in multiple interactions; negotiating conflict; or making decisions regarding policies and practices, a school leader has opportunity to appeal to shared values. Of course, this can only be done if values are shared and have been made explicit. In the process of appealing to shared values, the perceptive leader also must seize the opportunity to point out the unrecognized poetry, the awe, the beauty, the miracle of the everyday. They capitalize on every opportunity to stir the imagination, touch the heart, and inspire the soul.

While for many who work in schools job security, tenure, and favorable evaluations are important, just as important is their need for belonging and a sense of meaning, purpose, and significance. Paying attention to the whole person is vital to meeting their needs. Leaders who tap into the hopes, dreams, and aspirations of those they lead address these deeper inner needs, which when attended to, can result in more passionate engagement with one's work.

It is fairly common knowledge that people will aspire to higher standards of performance when they feel genuinely appreciated and recognized for their efforts. According to Kouzes and Posner (1999), encouragement increases the chance that people will actually achieve higher levels of performance. They offer seven practical actions for encouraging the heart: Set clear standards, expect the best, pay attention, personalize recognition, tell the story, celebrate together, and set the example. When imbued with poetic sensibilities, these actions can transform the nonchalant to the noble and lift the everyday to heights of deep significance.

Another important aspect of developing shared intentions and touching the heart is the use of symbols. People need items, stories, and rituals that become a pathway to meaning. Some symbols that appear simple or even corny can hold significant meaning to people who have been part of a particular experience. The power of symbols to engage people emotionally and in the meaning-making process makes them valuable tools for school leaders. Because change is often fraught with frustration and disillusionment, a leader's effective use of symbols can provide the bridge from familiar to unfamiliar, from the known to the unknown. This allows others to look at their everyday work with new eyes.

Literature and scripture, in particular, are rich with symbols. In discussing symbols, Rollins (1983) writes: "Beginning with the known, the scriptural symbol invites contemplation of the unknown. Using the familiar as a touchstone, it leads the reader to consideration of the unfamiliar. Commencing with facts and probabilities known to the conscious mind, it gestures toward possibilities intuited by the soul" (71). Particularly in times of crisis, leaders are looked upon to do likewise—to connect the new and strange with the familiar, to help make sense and meaning, and to give hope in the face of despair. Like scriptural symbol, poetry takes the reader down a similar path. A word or phrase familiar to the reader leads him or her to a deep emotional experience within a few lines.

When, for example, September 11, 2001, was catapulted into history from a simple block on the calendar to a date of epic proportion, staff, faculty, and students alike looked to principals to give hope. The event, replete with symbolism in such things as the date itself, 911, and what the Pentagon and the Twin Towers stood for, no doubt made a significant impact on the psyche of the nation.

As two major symbols of American culture, the Pentagon and the Twin Towers encoded a wide array of meanings that reflected this nation's beliefs, values, and practices. As powerful as these symbols have been, they were not on the minds of Americans as most of us went about our daily lives prior to September 11. Had some journalist, for instance, attempted to articulate the powerful nature of these two symbols, absent the associated tragedies, it would have most likely been considered unnecessary, perhaps even corny. Similarly, in schools, the taken-for-granted aspects of daily schooling can serve as powerful meaning makers in the face of ambiguity or crisis.

The perceptive leader identifies such symbols and presents them in ways that cultivate meaning. As Bolman and Deal (1991) see it, symbols play a powerful, vital, and complex role in the life of any group or organization. "They encode an enormous variety of meanings and messages into economical and emotionally powerful forms. They reflect and express an organization's *culture*—the pattern of beliefs, values, practices, and artifacts that define for its members who they are and how they do things" (250). It would be prudent for school leaders, cognizant of the deep-seated human needs in their schools, to actively seek out and develop the symbolic life of the school. The leader must be perceptive enough to identify, preserve, and even create events and activities that would serve as cultural cement to bring cohesiveness within the school. Establishing rituals and ceremonies, using metaphors, and even erecting visual symbols can provide the sense of cohesion.

Since human beings are emotional first and rational second, frequently the most important aspect of any event is not what happened, but what it means. Leaders must be insightful about this aspect of being human as they try to understand and practice the meaning-making aspect of their role. These considerations can help determine alternative approaches to problem solving, decision making, and communication. Given poetry's power to connect to human emotion, the poet's craft holds potential for broadening the range of approaches to problem solving, decision making, and communication in schools.

INSPIRING PERFORMANCE

Inspiring performance is another critical role of the school leader. If the human need for meaning in work life is to be met, leaders are key in helping to create that meaning. When leaders pay attention to meaning making as a vital function of their position, people can become inspired.

This idea of inspiring performance is underscored by Moxley (2000). He writes,

> There is an understanding and practice of leadership that elevates spirit, honors the whole self, and encourages us to use all of our energies in the activities of leadership . . . that taps into the best that is within us, that gives each

of us an opportunity to be involved and engaged . . . that helps us discover meaning in our work, that helps us live out our vision and make our mission manifest. It is an understanding that makes use of our spiritual energy, and it is understood as a spiritual experience. It leads to inspired performance. (10)

Inspiration resonates with hope, uplifted spirits, and passion. These are emotions that humans strive to enjoy every day. Since it is not uncommon to find school staff that is dispirited and apathetic, I would like to believe that an opportunity to enliven and emotionally engage people within schools would be embraced. I would also like to believe that attending to the spiritual needs that surface within schools will eventually become as comfortable as teaching reading is today.

By spirituality, I am not advocating any particular type of religious practice, as what it means to be spiritual is quite controversial. Here, I am simply referring to the ways in which school leaders can help meet the needs for meaning in work life by engaging those they lead on an emotional level. This has to do with cultivating practices within schools that help people feel valued, as part of a community to which they can bring their whole selves. It requires active engagement of the mind and the spirit in schoolwork.

This spiritual nature of work is also emphasized by Sergiovanni (1996), whose description of the leader's role as ministerial implies a dimension of spirituality and caretaking. He delineates eight tasks that are important to the formal leader in this moral realm: purposing, which refers to the leader's responsibility to create and align shared goals or guiding the community to articulate its values and beliefs; maintaining harmony; institutionalizing values; motivating; managing; enabling; modeling; and supervising.

In addition to fulfilling the need to manage effectively, the leader is called here primarily to help those they lead make sense of, and find meaning in, their work. This is not the kind of work that can be accomplished by a few cosmetic changes or actions. It requires a heartfelt passion and deep-seated commitment, an attentive attitude, masterful communication, and insightful action. To do so well, one must address issues of the heart, the soul, and the spirit. Each of these eight tasks, some to a greater degree than others, can be directly ennobled by some aspects of the poet's craft.

SELF-LEADERSHIP

The need for passion, commitment, attention, communication, and insight points out the sense-making and meaning-making role of the leader and also indicates a high level of emotional involvement with the work. The realities of life in public schools make for some unique conditions for leadership, and school leaders must, in addition to addressing the needs of others in the school, address needs in themselves. In other words, it is part of the ethical responsibility of leaders to be competent by striving to develop within themselves the skills and attitudes necessary to lead school well.

Whereas the explicit needs of the school can be attended to by delineating tasks and roles, the implicit needs of the school call for ongoing high levels of self-examination, self-honesty, and self-development. One must continually reexamine the self in terms of principles by which one lives and principles by which one attempts to lead. There must be congruence between the two. If one leads by a different set of principles than those by which one lives, the tasks of leading become infinitely more difficult. To lead a unified life, as opposed to a dichotomous life with two different sets of principles, is crucial to effective leadership. Leadership of the self, then, precedes leadership of others. Control of the self precedes control of others. Influence of the self precedes influence over others. We bring our selves to the tasks of leadership, and effective leadership is predicated on congruence among our thoughts, words, and actions.

Similarly, understanding of the self precedes understanding of others, empathy for the self precedes empathy for others, kindness toward oneself precedes kindness toward others, love for oneself precedes love for others, and care of the self precedes care for others. So who we are and what we value matter greatly in our attempts to lead. What leaders believe about themselves plays an important part in their ability to lead, and just as important is what a leader believes about others. An understanding of human nature is vital to effective leadership. Pellicer (1999) seems even more emphatic about this as he asks:

> Just what do you believe about people: What kinds of things do you say to them? What do you say about them? Do you see them as being essentially good and kind and caring in their dealings with others, or as evil, mean, and

nasty? Do you regard most people as being lazy or industrious? Selfish or giving? Boring or interesting? Dull or ingenious? The answers to these questions are critical because they define your personal philosophy and determine the parameters of how you will approach others in a leadership role, as well as how others will be inclined to respond to your attempts to lead. (21)

In short, our inner lives matter greatly in the work we do, because it is at that level we connect meaningfully with those we lead. It is in touching the heart, soul, and spirit that followers move from alienation, apathy, frustration, and disillusionment to commitment and hope. It is in acknowledging and acting on our understanding of human nature by addressing the whole person that we inspire others to do their best.

TOUCHING THE HEART, SOUL, AND SPIRIT

Separating spirit from work is a division as artificial as a division of the human body into parts. Each is connected and contributes to the effective functioning of the whole. Moxley (2000) points out that we are so adept at compartmentalizing our lives, that the notion of spirit as connected to work seems strange to many. Likewise, in discussing the inner life, Bolman and Deal (2002) remind us that the search for soul and spirit always has been central to the human experience, despite a modern tendency to shunt it aside. However, as previously mentioned, recent literature shows a distinct renewed interest in examining the spiritual side of work.

Although any discussion of spirituality in schools may feel awkward, the importance of its inclusion in discussing school leadership relates directly to the need for making meaning in schools, a need variously expressed by teachers and students alike. It is important to note here that since the events of September 11, before which time this manuscript was first drafted, the degree of discomfort at the mention of spirituality has certainly dissipated. However, confusion about the term *spirituality* exists. Vail (1998) explains that confusion about the term's meaning

comes from a powerful compound of strong but heterogeneous Judeo-Christian religious traditions and approaches, a burgeoning "new age" movement in which spirituality of some kind plays a central part, and a new interest in traditional non-Judeo-Christian religions and theologies.

Furthermore, in the West all this positive interest and fervor exists in perpetual tension with the tradition of religious freedom, with its accompanying suspicion that anyone who wants to discuss spirituality may secretly have some proselytizing to do, some souls to save. (177)

In post–September 11 America, the suspicion surrounding use of the term *spirituality* in schools may be lessening.

What is the meaning of spirituality? To answer this question, we turn to Vail's (1998) description of spirituality as

a decision to search somewhere else than in scientific findings and derived practices, secular support systems, or positive addictions like aerobic exercise, or in any other doctrines and technologies of human origin that purport to offer answers. Spirituality seeks fundamentally to get beyond materialistic conceptions of meaning. Spirituality is a decision to search beyond what one can do . . . to be spiritual is to try to turn away from all the props entirely and to open oneself to a transcendent source of meaning. (179)

Usually when the going gets tough, people rekindle their faith. Some basic questions come into sharp relief. Questions such as: What is life really about? Why exactly do I work? Am I doing what I'm here to do? This personal quest requires a deeper exploration of one's life, its meaning, and its purpose. Getting beyond the materialistic conceptions of meaning and opening oneself up to a transcendent source of meaning is a common everyday experience on an individual level as people deal with the challenges in their private lives. In the public arena, such ruminations tend to be shunted aside.

Traditionally, organizational structures provide ample room for physical bodies and require exercise of mental capabilities. They may even tolerate some emotion. However, they leave little or no room for spirit. In the words of Moxely (2000):

Once we realize that it is spirit that defines our self at the deepest levels of our being—that spirit enables us to offer our whole selves to the activity of leadership, to connect to others richly and rewardingly, and to give us deep sources of meaning—then we begin to understand its relationship to leadership and its importance to work. To the extent that we continue to turn attention away from matters of the spirit—that is, continue to believe that only physical, mental, and emotional energies are important at work—we go on ignoring a reality that could give new energy and vitality to us as individuals and our organizations. (8–9)

New energy and vitality are crucial to the improvement of schools. Here, the implications for leaders are evident. In school settings, attention is generally paid to the mental, the physical, and the emotional; the spiritual is often left unattended. This may be unfortunate, since the spiritual may be the very aspect of our lives that would be of most value in our quest for sense making and meaning making in uncertain, complex, and ambiguous environments.

Poets routinely connect the emotional and the spiritual to the physical and mental. They are adept at matters of the heart, soul, and spirit. These are definite aspects of their craft from which leaders can benefit. As we consider the possibility of navigating an uncertain future, we would be remiss if we were to ignore the value of qualities associated with the soul. We can see readily that poetry, from time immemorial, has been concerned mainly with issues of the heart, soul, and spirit—issues of meaning, memory, unity, and beauty. Incorporating them more fully into our conceptualization of leadership points to the value of poetry in a "destitute time."

Part 2

THE VALUE OF POETRY

This section explores the craft of poetry. There are perhaps as many definitions of poetry as there are poets, and this part of the book shares several of those definitions, including my own.

Here, too, several devices of poetry that can be beneficial to school leadership are discussed, as are the uses of poetry. The value of poetry to humanity beyond pure enjoyment is addressed. Poetry is presented as a form of communication and as a soul-making activity, and discussions about its ability to answer a primal urge and its role in providing knowledge and meaning complete the section and set the stage for introducing the usefulness of applying poetry techniques to school leadership roles.

Chapter Four

What Is Poetry?

Because it exists in so many forms, and on so many levels, poetry may be said to defy definition. Nonetheless, several attempts have been made. To answer the question What is poetry? one finds as many definitions as there are writers on the subject. In order to find utility in poetry, some definition would be necessary.

POETRY DEFINED

Definitions range from the simple and commonsense to the formal and elaborate. For example, Jerome (1984) defines poetry as writing that uses line breaks. That is, instead of continuing to the margin, you break the stream of words and place them where you please. This simple definition attends mainly to form. A more apt and useful definition would address issues of content.

Stauffer (1946) presents the idea that a poem is like a person, in that "each one is individual, unmistakable, and unduplicable" (15). He describes poetry as exact, intense, significant, concrete, complex, rhythmical, and formal. This description could serve useful in examining the value of the nature and content of poetry. Gioia (1992) defines poetry more succinctly as "an art—like painting or jazz, or opera or drama—whose pleasures are generally open to any intelligent person with the inclination to savor them" (xi). Inherent in this definition is an invitation that makes poetry accessible to any intelligent person.

The *American Heritage Dictionary* (1994) defines a poem as "a verbal composition characterized by the use of condensed language chosen for its sound and suggestive power and by the use of literary techniques such as meter and metaphor." This literal definition draws attention to the language of poetry, which warrants exploration for its value to leadership communication. Like the language of poetry, the language of leadership must be pleasing in sound, must possess some persuasive or suggestive power, and must communicate meaning.

Altenbernd and Lewis (1966) define poetry as "the interpretive dramatization of experience in metrical language." They then explain how poetry communicates in many ways at once: "Poetry employs several means of communication. . . . Each interacting with each other to produce a net effect greater than the impact of each component taken separately. For example, sentence structure, concreteness of detail, the meanings and associations of words, and implied dramatic situation all contribute to the total effect of the poem—to be experienced as a whole" (4–5). This description holds great potential for exploring the usefulness of poetry in leadership, especially the ability to communicate in many ways at once.

To Brooks and Warren (1965), poetry is organic in nature. They note:

> A poem is not to be thought of as merely a bundle of things which are "poetic" in themselves. Nor is it to be thought of, as a group of mechanically combined elements—meter, rhyme, figurative language idea, and so on—put together to make a poem as bricks are put together to make a wall. Rather, the relationship among the elements in a poem is what is all important; it is not a mechanical relationship but one which is far more intimate and fundamental. If we must compare a poem to the make-up of some physical object it ought not to be to a wall but to something organic like a plant. (16)

The organic nature of poetry described here, with its emphasis on relationship, enlarges our vision of the nature of poetry, beyond its technical qualities to the mood and spirit of poetry.

There is also a dramatic aspect to poetry, or *dramatic organization,* as Brooks and Warren term it. All poetry, they point out, involves a dramatic organization. "This is clear when we reflect that every poem implies a speaker of the poem, either the poet writing in his own person or someone into whose mouth the poem is put, and that the poem represents the reaction of such a person to a situation, a scene, or an idea. In this sense every poem can be—and in fact must be—regarded as a little drama" (20). This is a natural result of poetry, since it comprises the expression of the universality of human experience. And, what is more dramatic than the human experience? Here, too, the applicability to school leadership is clear in terms of the drama of life in schools.

The nature of poetry certainly allows for a variety of definitions, none of which are mutually exclusive. Taken together, they present poetry as a practical art form that resonates with the human experience. Its language as well as its spirit and mood are accessible and useful to us.

Perhaps Hillyer (1960) expresses it best:

> Poetry attempts to seize thoughts and emotions from the flow of time and shape them into something more lasting and beautiful than they were in the ordinary course of human experience. Observation and memory play equal parts in the selection of the thought and emotion, while the imagination, working at fiery intensity, selects one element to be expressed and burns away all irrelevant material that clings to it. At the same time, the poet is starting to frame the theme in words, heightening and condensing them, and setting them to a recurrent rhythm, a repetition of emphasis, such as we find at the basis of all natural things, the rotation of the planets, the ebb and flow of the sea, the turning of the seasons, the beat of our own hearts. The Universe has a vast rhythm of its own, to which the poet's ear is like a shell echoing the waves of the sea. (vii)

In my definition, poetry is communication that paints pictures that stir the imagination and employs strong, emotive language that touches the human heart and inspires the soul. This definition carries strong motivational undertones and underscores several aspects of poetry that are consonant with qualities necessary for effective leadership. Herein lies the primary value of poetry for leadership. Which leader does not need to stir imagination and use language in ways that inspire those they lead? Whether recognized or not, followers are looking for leaders who can inspire them.

When closely examined, the process of poetry (examining the environment, thinking deeply/reflecting, imagining, making connections, and communicating) as well as the product of poetry (the poems themselves, which demonstrate techniques of concise, effective, inspirational writing) can contribute immeasurably to leadership.

Poetry presents ideas concisely and imaginatively. In presenting a new idea or a new approach to an old idea, poets make significant use of emotional appeal. The ability and need to present new ideas or new approaches to old ideas are also hallmarks of effective leadership. In schools where new approaches to old ideas predominate, this ability of poets would be particularly useful. An exploration of the language and elements of poetry may help us glean some of the treasures buried in the art and craft of this art form.

THE LANGUAGE OF POETRY

Since communication is a hallmark of leadership, the language of poetry is of particular interest here. The power of poetry lies primarily in its language. Poetry has a tremendous impact on its reader or listener, which is achieved through use of imagery and figurative language such as metaphors, similes, and hyperbole.

One of the characteristics that distinguishes literature from nonliterary writing is literature's concern with conveying the emotion that accompanies an experience. Emotion can be conveyed through many vehicles, including the connotations of the words, the beat and pace of the rhythms, the associations surrounding the images, and the significance of the events narrated. All these elements come together to establish the emotional impact of poetic language. Poetry arouses a range of emotions. Some are negative, like anger, hate, and ridicule; others are positive, like love, enthusiasm, and laughter.

Poets are skillful in their use of words. One of the definitions examined earlier points out that poetry communicates in many ways at once. To achieve this, poets choose words appropriate to their purpose. This means they must exercise great care in selecting their words. But poetry looks deceptively easy. The language of poetry is condensed, compressed, and intense, and a reader must look for the overtones or suggestions as well as the literal meaning.

The selection of words in a poem, or its diction, then, is of utmost importance. Skelton (1956) explains that "whether the poem arouses one to delight or pain, to a realization of something new or startling, or to the appreciation of something long known beautiful, but now clearly seen for the first time; whether it fills one with horror or with amusement, the important factor of one's appreciation is the aptness of the words" (7). In a similar manner, effective leaders pay attention to the aptness of the words they choose to use to communicate with a particular audience. One would choose different words to inspire than to simply provide information.

Hillyer (1960), too, is quite attuned to the importance of diction. He writes:

> One measure of a poet's skill lies in his manipulation of the various shades of diction. Some words are prosaic, or 'flat,' and have no extra significance beyond their literal meaning as in the dictionary. But a large proportion of the words in any language imply emotions or ideas quite apart from their literal meanings. These implications we call suggestions or overtones and much of the effect of poetry resides in them. (9)

The skillful manipulation of diction is of utmost importance to school leaders whose role primarily consists of communication.

The ability to use both a word's denotative meaning, or dictionary definition, and its connotative meaning, which consists of the accumulation of emotional associations the word has gathered through its history or acquires in a given setting, would be valuable to one whose roles and tasks are primarily concerned with effective communication. The ability to go beyond the denotative meaning, by adding style, flavor, and perhaps humor, enables the leader to communicate attitudes, values, and dispositions.

Literal communication is not the sort that inspires, stirs the imagination of, or motivates others. Literal communication provides information. Literary communication, on the other hand, while providing information, is also a vehicle for inspiration. The language of poetry goes directly to the heart and makes a faster and stronger communication than prose. But not only does it touch the heart, it also touches the mind.

Take, for example, this prose statement: Whenever I see a rainbow in the sky, I get really excited. That began happening when I was a child and still continues today, even though I am grown. I hope I will feel this same excitement when I grow old; otherwise, I would prefer to be dead.

Now we can compare the ability of poetry to touch the heart and mind as this same sentiment is expressed by William Wordsworth's "My Heart Leaps Up."

> My heart leaps up when I behold
> A rainbow in the sky;
> So was it when my life began,
> So is it now I am a man,
> So be it when I shall grow old,
> Or let me die!

One can readily see that the language in verse has a much more powerful impact on the heart and mind than does prose. The use of figurative
language enables the poet to plumb the depths of human emotion. Imagery predominates the language of poetry and produces in the mind an
effect very nearly the same as that created by stimulation of the sensory
organs. Similes, metaphors, and personification are the most commonly
used forms of imagery or figurative language.

While poems, to some, may appear to be simple or nonsensical, they
usually hold profound meaning. That meaning may be simple and elegant
or elaborate and complicated. As one reads a poem, one finds a pattern of
sound. On closer examination one may detect the visual imagery. These
techniques of poetry work together to communicate on an emotional level.

The following is a favorite poem from my childhood, William
Wordsworth's "The Solitary Reaper."

> Behold her, single in the field,
> Yon solitary highland lass!
> Reaping and singing by herself;
> Stop here, or gently pass!
> Alone she cuts and binds the grain,
> And sings a melancholy strain;
> O listen! for the vale profound
> Is overflowing with the sound.

When I was a young girl, this first stanza held for me a special appeal.
Perhaps it was because it resonated with my pastoral existence in the
countryside, where I frequently ventured out into the field by myself. Here
Wordsworth gives tremendous charm and novelty to ordinary life. His
verse allowed me to see my routine, everyday existence with new eyes.
With fresh poetic imagery, he allowed me to see the unrecognized poetry
in my mundane existence.

Imagery in poetry serves various functions. Imagery provides setting,
stimulates the imagination, allows us to see ordinary objects as we have
never seen them before. Imagery serves to glorify the commonplace and
the everyday in life to universal heights.

A dominant emotion, such as courage, love, faith, joy, indignation,
anger, admiration, or compassion, is usually evident in a poem. The poet
conveys these through devices such as rhythm, meter, imagery, and allu-

sion, as well as through the use of words that have emotional connotations. An effective leader would at some level decide on what he or she wants to convey and craft the communication accordingly.

Poets pay particular attention to the means by which the ideas are conveyed. Aside from a few explicit, literal statements, poets mainly use figurative language to link two things, attending simultaneously to the concrete and the abstract, the literal and the figurative, the near at hand and the far or absent, the tangible and the intangible. They continually appeal to the senses and make their statements and convey their ideas through comparisons. The poem "Valley Ecstasy," which follows, demonstrates the poet's skill at conveying a particular emotion, in this instance, joy. By crafting his communication with rhythm, imagery, and other poetic devices, the poet turns the ordinary into the extraordinary, seeing beauty in what could easily be seen as common or matter-of-fact.

Valley Ecstasy

It was early in the morning as I walked
along the way,
The sun was rising in the East reflecting
in the bay,
All nature was so quiet, yet vibrant
as could be,
The birds began their sweet refrain
apparently for me.
I heard an owl up in a tree calling
for his mate,
He looked at me as if to say, the world is
full of hate.
I saw his lover as she came and perched up
in a branch,
They both looked down as if to say we're filled
with love and mirth.
I walked along that rugged path near the waters
of the lake,
The lake so calm and quiet it made
my spirit quake.
My thought of mysteries of life as I strolled
along that day,

> The things that mean so much to us and brighten
> up the way,
> My mind continued musing on the beauties
> of the dawn,
> As I came across a baby deer known
> as a fawn.
> I thought of those forsaken, so lonely
> and forlorn,
> And wished that they could be with me this bright
> and glorious morn.
> I do not like to leave this place so quiet
> and so still,
> But I must journey onward and travel
> up the hill;
> For up there too there's peace and joy and gladness
> and good will,
> As I look down in the valley, and see the flowers
> and the rill.

—Reverend Arnold R. Vail

From a simple story-like beginning with rhythm and rhyme, the poet pulls us into his world. We feel his joy, his longing, and his need to continue his journey. He skillfully merges imagination and memory. By juxtaposing the stillness of the dawn with the busyness of his mind as it flits from the mysteries of life to the lonely and then to his need to continue his journey, the poet evokes a sense of motion and emotion. He gives deep significance to a quiet morning, turning a simple activity into an uplifting and enchanting moment of existence.

The power of figurative language lies in relating one thing to something else, as in relating the conditions in a school to a snake pit or to a rose garden. The relationship and the effects produced by establishing it can astonish, incite, delight, or motivate. In essence, figurative language can invoke any number of emotions. The metaphor is an implied likeness, in that it speaks of one object in terms of another, or as if the object were the other. The metaphor of school as a snake pit certainly conjures up a different set of images and elicits different emotions than the metaphor of school as a rose garden.

When similarity, rather than identity, is asserted, using the word *like* or *as*, the figure of speech being used is a simile. When a metaphor is much extended, and especially when the poet develops a narrative out of a complex of subordinate metaphors derived from the main one, the result is an allegory. Sometimes poets use hyperbole, which is a deliberate, and often outrageous, exaggeration, to magnify a fact or an emotion in such a way as to attribute great importance to it. Use of understatement, the opposite of hyperbole, which is usually ironic, is also common.

Personification, used when an object is attributed with the characteristics of a human being, can be quite useful in helping people understand change. Language in poetry is also used to convey sound value and tone. Some sound values in poetry come in the form of rhyme; alliteration, which is the repetition of a sound; or the imitation of a natural sound, which is known as onomatopoeia.

Tone in a poem expresses attitudes. Similarly, in speaking, the tone of a conversation indicates the speaker's attitude toward the subject and toward the audience. Often the true meaning is communicated not by the literal words but by the tone in which something is said. For example, the simple word *sure* can mean anything from wholehearted agreement to arrogance and condescension, depending on the tone in which it is uttered. Similarly, in written communication, the writer must depend on the written words to take the place of the intonations and expressiveness of the human voice. The writer must choose and arrange the words so that they convey to the reader the desired tone, with all the understated meanings. Tone is of importance to leaders, whether it is in verbal or written communication.

THE CONTENT OF POETRY

Poetry is certainly not solely an expression of emotion. Although emotions seem to dominate poetry, poetry does much more than gush with sentimentality. Sometimes the poet concentrates on an idea rather than on an image, appealing less to the imagination and emotion and more to the mind. The poet transforms an idea into powerful verse, as in the 19th-century English poet Shelley's sonnet "Ozymandias," in which he presents a powerful picture of the temporal nature of people and things as an intellectually significant idea in the poem. While the idea predominates, deep emotion is still present. Presented together, emotions and ideas strengthen each other.

When imbued with emotion, ideas are communicated much more powerfully, touching the head and the heart simultaneously. Emotion serves to
intensify the idea, while the idea serves to give intellectual significance to
the emotion. A poem usually tells a story or communicates an idea. The
poet decides whether the idea or the emotion should dominate the poem. A
touching poem usually comprises an interplay between idea and emotion.

In order to communicate more effectively, to give more depth and
meaning, poets often do not tell the story in a straightforward manner as
in prose. They use imagery and figurative language devices to permeate
their work with meaning. The poet usually arranges the story within specific devices of emphasis, such as the use of vivid wording, emphatic
phrasing, or climactic position. The story is set within or against the emotion, idea, or character portrait.

Because ideas are central to the poem, it is worth repeating that poems
do much more than gush with sentiments. However, the presence of sentiments is precisely what makes the idea more meaningful and memorable. Poets memorialize ideas by positioning them amid emotions. Embodied in sense data, ideas are lifted to a higher plane and become much
more comprehensive than when they are expressed without emotion.

Poems usually recount some aspect of the human experience, and as
such, themes can be readily evident within them. Often, historical context
is embodied in a poem, and one can connect a poem to the prevailing
views of its time.

To embody ideas, poets make liberal use of symbols. The symbol will
usually evoke the emotions that surround the symbolized object. Allu-
sions, myths, and archetypes are common symbols used in poetry. An allusion, which usually serves to reinforce and illustrate the writer's point,
is a reference without lengthy explanation, to literature, history, or current
events. Allusion may be used to show the similarity of the human experience through different periods of history. Myth, a narrative telling of the
exploits of gods or heroes, often serves to deepen meaning in the narrative
of a poem. Archetypes, the frequent recurrence from the earliest times to
the present of a number of themes, situations, narratives, and character
types, are usually rendered through dramatic symbols drawn from the author's own time. Repeated motifs, or archetypes, such as the search for a
father, the Oedipus complex, dying and rebirth, and the night journey, also
figure prominently in poetry as a basis for vivid narrative.

Drawing on the power of archetypes can serve to add substance, deeper meaning, connection, and a sense of history to ideas that are being communicated. Archetypes exert strong emotional appeal to readers and listeners. Samuel Taylor Coleridge's "The Rime of the Ancient Mariner," one of the most famous long story poems in the English language, holds a treasury of poetic effects, but is dominated by supernatural elements. Similarly, there are poets such as Edgar Allan Poe and Walter de la Mare whose poems deal with pure fantasy or imaginary events. I am much more interested here in poetry that deals with actual events; for example, the two previously referenced poems by William Wordsworth and Arnold Vail.

Given the strength of the interplay of ideas and emotion in poetry, this form of communication lends itself to various uses. In the case of school leadership, the need to provide information as well as inspiration makes some aspects of the poet's craft viable tools for enhanced communication.

Chapter Five

Uses of Poetry

Extraordinary claims have often been made for poetry. Matthew Arnold saw poetry as capable of saving mankind. While Arnold's view may be somewhat hyperbolic, poetry is of great use to us. Dating from antiquity, poetry has been used to communicate deep feelings, to intensify our power of observation, and to stir our imagination. The remarkable qualities of poetry touch the emotions deeply and alert the mind vividly, thereby making the art form accessible and of immense value and use. Untermeyer, Ward, and Stauffer (1938) adeptly sum up the uses of poetry: "From the beginning of time, hope has been sustained, grief has been alleviated, memory has been strengthened, and anger has been transformed through poetry. It might be said that the chief use of poetry is the ability to communicate emotion—*all* the emotions" (153).

Skelton (1956) credits C. Day Lewis with defining the poet's task, which is "to recognize pattern wherever he sees it, and to build his perceptions into a poetic form which by its urgency and coherence will persuade us of truth" (7). The role of persuading others of what is inherently true of the world or of mankind demands a certain perceptual skill. The ability to conduct this vital, specialized task should not be underestimated. It requires seeing beyond the superficial, beyond the facade, and beyond surface appearances. It requires seeing in the mundane the majesty and grandeur of life.

Insight, attention, and perspective are critical here. Having recognized what is uplifting, what is noteworthy, and what is useful, one has to then find the most effective way of communicating these insights. Here, the poet's eye and the poet's pen serve as moral agents—relaying to us what is true about our lives and our experiences.

Perhaps poetry has prevailed through the ages because of its role in expressing the essence of the human experience. There is a certain element of universality in poetry that makes it accessible and useful in enriching all our endeavors.

Most simply put, in my estimation, poetry taps into our emotions, connects them with experience, and presents them in words for us to examine, relive, and enjoy. That poetry is a mirror would be my most apt metaphor here. But poetry is more than a mirror that reflects only the tangible, surface appearances. It is a special kind of mirror that reflects the intangible, the abstract, and matters of the heart, the soul, and the spirit. In so doing, it makes itself accessible for our use, particularly in examining our hidden needs—needs for meaning and purpose.

I see poetry as a tool for enlivening, elevating, exalting, and enriching the human experience with exceptional acuity. As poets ply their craft, the emotional intensity is quite evident. Its attunement to the rhythms of life, such as the rise and fall of the tides, the revolutions of the earth and other planets, even to our own heartbeats, sets it in a class by itself, where it has access to our inner selves, and we likewise have access to it.

The notion of poetry in everyday use, then, appears quite practical. Keen observation allows us glimpses of the unrecognized poetry that crowds our daily lives. Two arenas of daily life in which poetry may prove of practical use are in our communication and spiritual expression.

COMMUNICATION

Matthew Arnold is credited with saying that poetry is "simply the most beautiful, the most impressive, and the most effective mode of saying things" (as cited in Untermeyer et al., 1938, 49). Of course, being a poet he was probably biased toward his craft. However, I tend to agree that prose just never comes across with the same impact as verse. Perhaps Samuel Taylor Coleridge put it most succinctly when he said, "Prose: words in their best order. Poetry: the *best* words in the best order" "(as cited in Untermeyer et al., 1938, 49). Coleridge emphasizes the point by referring to both the content and the form.

In spite of its critics, poetry has been a persistent form of communication down through the ages. In addition to being the oldest and perhaps the most powerful of the arts, there are several other advantages that poetry has over verse. Untermeyer et al. (1938) delineates five of them in this way:

> (1) Because of its strongly pronounced rhythm and constant beat, poetry, far more rapidly than prose, stirs our feelings, stimulates our minds, and awakens our memories. (2) Because of its tighter pattern and shorter line, poetry condenses into a firmer shape. Thus we can more easily understand and remember the central idea. (3) Because of the elevated pitch and rousing tone, poetry is a more effective medium for the communication of emotion; it intensifies our experiences and associations. (4) Because it is more dramatic than prose, it expresses information with more speed and color; even facts are revealed in a new way when poetry lifts them out of their common setting and brings them into bold relief. (5) Because of its image-making power, it colors familiar objects with novelty, adds suggestion to statement, and transforms the everyday world with unexpected pictures and quickening beauty. (34)

Poetry communicates much more powerfully than prose. It conveys tone and feeling through the precise use of words. This makes poetry a unique form of communication with special qualities. Although what we experience as readers or listeners of poetry is not necessarily exactly what the poet experienced, what is important is the meaning we derive from what we have heard or read. Something in the poetic material resonates with us or makes sense to us. As each person brings their experience to the material, the same poetic information may convey different meanings to different people. This malleable quality of poetry not only makes it accessible to everyone, but just as important, it makes it a viable vehicle for meaning making.

Eliot (1933) places a poem's existence somewhere between the writer and the reader. "A poem," he says, "is not just either what the poet 'planned' or what the reader conceived, nor is its 'use' restricted wholly to what the author intended or to what it actually does for readers" (31). This view of poetry speaks to the power resulting from the elements of poetry, such as technique, mood, and spirit, and presents it as a boundaryless, malleable, communication tool, which could be of inestimable value and use. Conscious and careful use of poetic devices can enliven communication and make it more effective.

Poetry can also be considered as a form of speech. While the difference between poetic speech and other forms of speech may seem to be more readily apparent than the similarities, the differences should not be allowed to hide the basic similarity. Essentially, in poetry, as in all other discourse, one person is saying something to another person. Understanding of this basic element of communication will enable us to better explore the differences in form and even search for ways to use some of the heretofore misunderstood or underused aspects of poetry.

Some of the nonverbal aspects of communication are captured by emphasis, rhythm, rhyme, and word choices that appeal to the heart as well as to the mind. Many people throughout history have used the techniques of poetry to make writing vivid, memorable, and inspiring.

In advertising, for example, techniques of poetry are used repeatedly to capture readers' attention. Rather than relying on just facts, advertisers appeal to specific audiences by associating their product with the perceived needs, wants, desires, and interests of each particular group. Their persuasion and influence frequently use appeals to authority, patriotism, and religion. Through the media, everyday people with absolutely no interest in literature are using or are being influenced by literary techniques and appeals.

The practicality of this present age notwithstanding, persuaders have not relented in their quest to influence the human mind. In fact, it appears that persuasion has intensified as the new economy drives businesses to find faster, better, and more cost-effective ways to compete for consumers' attention and money. Ironically, it could probably be said that ordinary persons, awash in competition for their minds, are somewhat oblivious to it.

While the words we use are important, just as important are the tonal characteristics of our voice and our body language. Even in simply conveying information, attitudes, feelings, and dispositions are evident. Pure exact information is hardly ever communicated without an attendant effect, which in turn colors the meaning of what is being said. Gestures, tone of voice, and facial expression all serve to communicate. Yet poets are able to convey full, total communication through the use of language.

Congruence among all three of these facets of communication results in effective communication. Lack of congruence, on the other hand, sends mixed messages and leaves the other person experiencing cognitive dissonance. With incongruence, one is not perceived as believable and one's credibility is at stake.

In poetry, one finds similar elements at work. Words, tone, and mood are all communicated on the printed page. The elements of poetry that create this powerful form of communication are worth examining for their everyday usefulness.

Essentially, poetry as a powerful form of communication engages both writer and reader, or speaker and listener, in meaning making. As such, techniques of poetry could be immensely useful in building powerful communication in areas of life and work in which meaning making is vital.

Effective communication is about getting in touch with one's true core, paying attention to the needs of the other person, listening and watching beyond the surface words, and using persuasion to help both parties of the communication get what they really want. Brooks and Warren (1965) ask us to remember that "poetry is not a thing separate from ordinary life and that the matters with which poetry deals are matters with which the ordinary person is concerned . . . it is highly important to see that both the impulse and methods of poetry are rooted very deep in human experience, and that formal poetry itself represents, not a distinction from, but a specialization of, thoroughly universal habits of human thinking and feeling" (7–8).

Poetry, then, is not to be viewed solely as an art form for the artistic or esoteric few. Rather, it can be explored and used in practical ways, in both our work and private lives. Furthermore, this creative, unifying, and dynamic art form can be explored in ways that could shed light on our understanding of our own nature and for its deeper spiritual value.

SPIRITUAL EXPRESSION

While the popularity of verse might have declined and the primal urges of the human heart might have been pushed underground, perhaps by the increasing acquisition of wealth, the need for meaning in life is ever present. We could be well served to examine and use, where we can, the elements of poetry that have resonated with the primal urge of the human heart in earlier centuries.

Apart from the utilitarian purpose of poetry, there is also a deeper emotional/spiritual use of poetic form. As Jerome (1984) explains it, "Your reason for writing poetry has something to do with the special nature of what you want to express. You want to write it down, more for yourself than for others, and for some strange reason prose just

doesn't feel right. You have an urge, which you may not quite understand yourself, to use broken lines. Usually, those who have that urge
have been moved by strong emotions, such as love, hate, sorrow, or appreciation of beauty" (8).

Each of us might be somewhat of a poet. Since prose seems inadequate
as a vehicle for expressing our intense emotions. It takes too long. It
seems too flat. Poetry is much more flexible than prose when it comes to
communicating emotion. Through the pattern, the spacing, the abrupt end-
ings, the rhythms, and the rhymes, the form of poetry lends itself well to
intensity of expression. Intense emotion demands an intense form of expression, the nature of which tends to assuage, temper, and accommodate
strong emotion. The nature of poetry is such that it can also exalt, uplift,
and ennoble whatever it touches.

What possible relevance does this archaic art form have to contemporary society? In light of the demands on school leaders and the context in
which they operate, possessing some of the skills inherent in the poet's
craft and the ability to pay attention to the environment, develop insight,
and ennoble the human spirit may be useful. Furthermore, the poet's ability to recognize patterns may offer insights into ways in which school
leaders can enhance their insight and attention in dealing with challenges
in the environment.

The challenges of the new millennium certainly require thinking outside the box. The complex nature of schools, coupled with the scope and
alacrity of change, demands that school leaders go beyond traditional
thought patterns and explore new realms. Perhaps some poetic treatment
applied to schools may hold the potential to exalt schooling in ways that
will better meet the human need for meaning.

Chapter Six

The Value of Poetry

Amid the affluence of the 21st century, poetry may be considered more ornamental than utilitarian. However, it is precisely in a time such as this that poetry may be most valuable. Written eight decades ago, and highly relevant today, T. S. Eliot's "The Wasteland," which portrays a spiritually desolate society in the 1920s, could be easily viewed as a depiction of modern American society. Poetry such as Eliot's tends to go beyond the everyday routines, stirring the imagination and helping to create a vision of the future.

Similarly, Hölderlin's (whose poem "Bread and Wine" inspired this work) use of bread and wine, items routinely used for daily sustenance, yet symbols of the divine, poignantly exemplifies the poet's ability to use insight and attention to turn the everyday into the sublime, touching the hearts and minds at a much deeper level, and thereby contributing meaningfully to the human spirit.

Brooks and Warren (1965) point out that because poetry has a basis in common human interests, the question of the value of poetry is to be answered by saying that it springs from a basic human impulse and fulfills a basic human interest. Poetry, then, is not an isolated and eccentric thing, but emanates from the most fundamental interests of human beings.

Because poetry can change a dull statement into a fresh and striking one, or transform a routine activity into an exciting endeavor, we need to consider a much wider use of this art form and engage audiences that today need the art most desperately. We need to tap into the value inherent in poetry that is not only of interest to poets, but is of use to all humans.

The culture, the technology, the way of life, the thinking might have changed, but the needs of the human heart have not changed with the dawn of the 21st century. Although poetry's cultural importance in the 18th and 19th centuries has given way to prose, the devices of poetry are still of immense value in this present age. Perhaps its use may be most valuable as ways of thinking, analyzing situations, making connections, and appealing to the needs of the human heart. Because poetry's existence as a form of art in some ways relates to our existence, poetry might be more necessary and its value even greater today than in the past.

One of the oldest art forms, poetry has successfully threaded its way throughout human civilization, connecting invisible strands of humanity that resonate from one generation to another, one era to the next, and one heart to another. There must be much more to poetry than meets the eye, and it is incumbent on us to reexamine the art and cull what it has to offer us today.

Poetry has the potential to add value to our existence in several ways, three of which will be explored here: soul making, answering the primal urge, and providing us with knowledge and meaning.

SOUL MAKING

From the earliest expression of joy, when hunters celebrated success, verse has had the power to stir the senses, touch the heart, and quicken the pulse. This unique power of poetry makes it much more valuable than we might have previously considered.

Since poetry appeals not only to the ear but to the eye, it is one of the most powerful art forms. It connects with the human spirit in such a profound manner that ordinary people use it in everyday life, knowingly or unknowingly. People use poetry for inspiration, for comfort, to memorize something, or to make a point stronger, particularly in times of peak emotion, such as sadness, loss, happiness, or excitement. At times when too much verbiage would dilute the power of the communication, when something has to be communicated quickly and poignantly, poetry is most comforting to the soul.

Drawing attention to this soul-making quality of poetry, Hirsch (1999) writes: "The poem of high spiritual attainment has the power, the almost magical potential, to release something that dwells deep within us. It taps into something that we otherwise experience haphazardly or at unlikely, decisive moments in our lives" (244). Some poems generate a sense of overpowering spirituality. This soul-making quality is probably most evident in the psalms, which deliver strong spiritual messages in verse.

But soulfulness emanates even from poems that are not overpoweringly spiritual. Take for example, the first and last verses of William Wordsworth's "I Wandered Lonely as a Cloud":

> I wandered lonely as a cloud
> That floats on high o'er vales and hills,
> When all at once I saw a crowd,
> A host, of golden daffodils;
> Beside the lake, beneath the trees,
> Fluttering and dancing in the breeze.
>
> For oft, when on my couch I lie
> In vacant or in pensive mood,
> They flash upon that inward eye
> Which is the bliss of solitude;
> And then my heart with pleasure fills,
> And dances with the daffodils.

Even without an overpowering sense of spirituality, one can experience a sense of delight in the first stanza. By the last stanza, the soulfulness is evident, where the initial delight has become a recurring cheerfulness to be experienced time and time again, even when the poet is in a pensive mood. The vivid memory enriches the soul.

Although the word *soul* is not as commonly used today as in previous eras, the soul has been used commonly as a literary device for transcendence. It may very well be the word, or concept du jour of the 21st century, particularly more so since the events of September 11, 2001, and the grave and growing global threats with the ensuing yearning for meaning in life and work and attention to things spiritual.

Recently, the heart, the soul, and spirit have all been resurfacing as viable constructs through which to view life and particularly for consideration by leaders as they seek to help provide meaning in the work life of those they lead. Whereas the idea of soul and spirit might seem quaint or irrelevant, the concepts cause you to think deeply, ponder, go beyond your physical self to a source of power greater than yourself.

In organizations, there has always been a need for pragmatic, results-driven decision making. However, that does not preclude the stirring of the heart and soul in the workplace. School leaders are asked to be results-driven: to increase test scores, to make decisions based on hard data. These all have their place, but the need for delivering better human beings must not be neglected in the process. In this endeavor, along with hard scientific data, sense data have a major role to play and should be used more widely in problem solving, in decision making, and in communication. Poetry has proved itself to be of value to the human soul by transcending across time and across cultures.

ANSWERING THE PRIMAL URGE

The power that poetry has exuded across time and across cultures speaks to a common if not primitive or primal urge of the human heart and soul. Referring to poetry, Hillyer (1960) makes a simple, yet profound statement: "With this key Mankind unlocked his heart" (2). He explains that the reader responds with his memory, in which are experiences and emotions similar to those expressed in the poem, and with his imagination, which is stimulated by rhythm and phrasing. Similarly, Hirsch (1999) observes that poems communicate before they are understood, and the structure operates on, or inside, the reader even as the words infiltrate the consciousness. Memory and imagination play a vital role in poetry.

Human memory and imagination connect with poetry and, in so doing, make particular kinds of meaning possible. Poetry, as a result, serves to facilitate access to some under-explored aspects of our selves. While the primal urge or some primitive joy may not be openly expressed in this postmodern era, its lack of overt presence does not deny its existence, or the need to attend to it.

By offering their craft to the public, poets serve the vital function of helping us to create meaning. It is up to us to find and use the value in poetry. Poetry helps us make sense of otherwise meaningless experiences. In other words, it enlightens us, gives us insights into our own existence. It allows us to bring order and meaning to what are otherwise construed as random or mysterious experiences.

Poetry has the potential to allow us greater access to ourselves, and to others; to inspire, and to be inspired. *Inspiration* is a term frequently associated with poetry. However, for some poetry enthusiasts, poetry goes beyond inspiration to intoxication. As Hirsch (1999) describes it, "We ought to speak of the poem that desires to sweep the reader away, to take the reader. Of reading as a form of sensual pleasure, a mode of possession, a method of travel. Of reading as a voluptuous and jubilant practice with its own ruthless will to the language of joy. Poetry is a devouring passion. Rapture testifies: I am reading my way into a state of enchantment and exultation, a state of bliss" (115).

If poetry can inspire such sentiments, and provide this kind of access, there must be something in the nature of poetry that can not only bring joy into our lives every day, but also benefit us in destitute times as well. Perhaps it is worthwhile to explore poetry for what it holds that is of concern to humanity rather than just of concern to poets.

Since schools are primarily about people and relationships, school leaders, like poets, are required to rise above the fray of the everyday to inspire and encourage the human heart. The use of poetic techniques in school leadership might lend itself not only to effective use of time and enhanced communication, but also to the acknowledgment of one's own humanity and the humanity of others. It can be used to attend to the soul and the spirit, to uplift, ennoble, and to inspire.

KNOWLEDGE AND MEANING

While inspiration is quite evident as a value of poetry, knowledge and meaning might be less evident. But poetry is not all about emotion; it also engages the intellect and appeals to the mind. Knowledge is not only of a scientific nature. For, whereas science describes the world in terms of verifiable evidence, poetry describes the intangible aspects of our world.

Feelings, matters of attitude, and idiosyncrasies are valid aspects of the human experience that do not fall within the realm of science. Poetry captures well these aspects of human experience and mirrors them back in recognizable form to its audience. The totality of the human experience cannot be explained in objective, observable, verifiable, scientific terms. When contrasted with the value of science, poetry has different objectives, and what makes science valuable cannot be held to make poetry valuable. Poetry attends to aspects of the human experience outside the realm of science. Science is methodical and is concerned with precision. The range of human experience far exceeds what is verifiable, observable, and scientific.

The kind of knowledge that poetry generates is qualitatively different from what we commonly refer to as knowledge—the factual, quantifiable kind. Craft and artistry with words chosen for their clarity and precision reflect the important aspects of human experience. Words are used to bring strength to the thought. Poetry gives us experiential knowledge that stimulates a different level of meaning than science does. The human effort to derive meaning from experience is greatly aided by poetry. Poetry provides us knowledge of ourselves and how we relate to the world. Innumerable poems relate our understanding of life, our participation in it, and our response to it. Some poetry appeals less to the emotion and imagination and more to the mind in cases where the thought or idea is put into powerful verse.

Increased understanding of poetry's role in revealing our nature allows us to see a much larger role for the poet's craft in our life and work. Poetry presents patterns of human nature and human existence and enables us to perceive ourselves in relation to the rest of humanity. Increased understanding of one's own nature is of inestimable value in creating meaning.

Due to its ability to help establish knowledge and meaning within oneself, between people, and even among nations, poetry should not be separated from our day-to-day communication. To get the full benefit of poetry, we must regard poetry not as an occasional phenomenon, but as a means toward developing meaning and knowledge in our everyday lives.

Brooks and Warren (1965) insightfully draw our attention to the idea that quite often talk that is apparently practical really attempts to satisfy a nonpractical interest. They write:

> It is easy to point out many other aspects of our experience that testify to the fact that people—even people who think that they care nothing for poetry—really have interests which are the same as those satisfied by poetry. Very few people indeed depend for the satisfaction of these interests merely on their routine activities. Instead, they listen to speeches, go to church, view television programs, read magazine stories or the gossip columns of newspapers. Such people do not see any relation between these activities and poetry, but poetry does concern the same impulses and the same interests. (21)

The connections between humans and poetry run even deeper. Poetry involves repetition and rhythm, just as the recurrent aspects of our lives and our world. Our hearts beat in recurrences. The ebb and flow of the tides, the stars in their courses, and the changing seasons are all evidence of a certain metrical quality to our existence. Additionally, in our everyday speech, we communicate our ideas with far more than just words. We communicate a host of emotions and attitudes right along with our ideas. From this perspective, poetry is evident in everyday places not usually considered poetic. One perks up at the use of alliteration in a speech or sermon or in a particularly resonant editorial piece or newspaper article.

But, one does not passively avail oneself of this knowledge that poetry yields. One has to be actively engaged in the larger spiritual nature of life. One way to do this is to pay attention to life and to be keenly observant. When one takes the time to observe, the dull takes on new life, the matter-of-fact becomes poignant, and the old seems new. A new level of meaning becomes evident, as the emotion is stirred and the imaginative impulse is awakened.

Webster's definition of a poet is one who demonstrates great imaginative power, insight, or beauty of expression. These very attributes are frequently ascribed to great leaders: thoughtful, insightful, and masterful communicators. I trust that school leaders will have the inclination to savor not only the pleasures of poetry but will put to use those aspects of the art and craft of poetry that are viable tools in the job of leading schools.

While poetry is used as a generic name for poems taken together, it is also used "to describe the spirit or mood which may find expression in, say, a painting or a piece of music" (Stauffer, 1946, 12). There is, then, the poetic spirit, and there is the poem. In this book, I am primarily using the term *poetry* to describe the mood or spirit that might find expression in a painting or a piece of music. I am also exploring how that same mood or spirit can find expression in leadership, and ways in which some of the technical qualities of poetry can enhance a leader's work.

Today, poetry is perhaps the most misunderstood of all the arts. The average adult is ambivalent, uncomfortable, or bored when faced with a poem. With the growth of visual communication, the eye has displaced the ear as the instrument for literary communication. But poetry is a rich mine to be tapped by anyone desiring to enrich their life.

To further explore some of the riches in poetry, I turn to five arguments Stauffer (1946) sets forth for poetry. The first is that a poem is like a person, in that each one is individual, unmistakable, and can't be duplicated. The second, that poetry is intense, refers to the passion and the emotion that poetry generates. The third claim is that poetry is significant in that it has something worthwhile to communicate. The fourth claim is that poetry is concrete in that the poets see their thoughts, in that sense data is connected to an image. The fifth claim is that poetry is complex in that it is an interplay of sensation, intellect, emotion, desire, and conscience.

Taken together, these five claims of uniqueness, intensity, significance, concreteness, and complexity are as applicable to school leadership as they are to poetry. The uniqueness of each person, interest group, or stakeholder with whom school leaders interact, as well as the uniqueness of the situations with which they struggle, make a strong case for attributing the term *uniqueness* to school leadership. Similarly, the intensity of the daily interactions, the need for significance and the significance of events, the need to be concrete as opposed to being vague or abstract, as well as the complexity of school life all lend themselves to interpretation and analysis through poetic lenses.

Part 3

THE RELEVANCE OF POETRY IN SCHOOL LEADERSHIP

Part 3 of the book attempts to bring the first two sections of the book together by discussing how school leaders can use poetry in their work.

The idea of perceptive leadership is introduced as a model for leading with insight, attention, and enhanced communication. The usefulness of poetry in informing the practice of school leadership is explored, and a professional development framework is proposed for developing poetic sensibilities.

This section ends with an epilogue imploring the reader to consider the utility of poetry in school leadership.

Chapter Seven

Perceptive Leadership

As can be seen from earlier discussion, we live in an age in which we need to honor a multiplicity of leadership perspectives in order to develop greater awareness and foster deeper understanding and sensitivity to the unique circumstances facing school leaders. One would be hard-pressed not to notice that the recent threat of terrorism does have a tremendous impact on schools and those who work in them. Likewise, other social, economic, political, and technological issues impact schools significantly.

The challenges of the present age demand perceptive leaders. In this decade it is not enough to reflect. It is critically important to perceive, to pay attention intensely in order to discern from the plethora of information and activity what is educationally significant, to develop new insights, and to communicate in ways that generate meaning. At the heart of this idea of perceptive leadership is the requirement that leaders become acutely attentive to the needs of those they lead, insightful about the context in which they operate, and effective in their communication.

The *American Heritage College Dictionary* defines *perceive* as "to become aware of directly through any of the senses, especially sight or hearing; to achieve understanding of; or to apprehend." The first phrase in this definition speaks to becoming aware. One should not ignore the importance of paying attention. In order to become aware, one must pay attention. This is the starting point of perception.

In schools, where life moves at a rapid pace, one cannot develop knowledge and engender meaning if one does not pay attention to what is taking place. It is a feeble existence, if one does not take some time to see some beauty in the mundane. Looking beyond the surface can produce new levels of insights that can lead to deeper levels of knowledge and meaning.

Reflective practice is discussed at length in the literature on school leadership. While the ability to reflect is extremely valuable, the ability to perceive is perhaps invaluable today. There is no doubt that it is important to pay attention to what has happened, and what is happening. My premise here is that it is as important to pay attention forward—to pay attention to what is likely to happen—as it is to pay attention to what has already happened. Leaders need to be able to understand how elements in the environment are changing, to determine which elements will impact the school, to formulate a response to the phenomenon, and to think ahead.

PERCEPTIVE PRACTICE

Three major tasks of leadership—decision making, problem solving, and communication—are becoming increasingly challenging as global changes create a more complex environment from which to draw information. The leader needs to be attentive, insightful, and articulate. Discernment is crucial.

Simply put, the perceptive leader pays attention to the environment, gathers information, examines issues from a multiplicity of perspectives, analyzes the information, makes connections, and develops new insights, which are then communicated in ways that engender understanding and meaning. As illustrated in figure 7.1, this three-part framework of poetic attention, insight, and literary communication are interrelated processes that enable leaders to conduct the three major leadership tasks of decision making, problem solving, and communication more meaningfully.

Poetic Attention

Poetic attention is concerned with intensity of focus. It is the poet's way of looking at the world, of apprehending the world to discover what is of significance. This intense attention leads to insight.

Poetic attention enhances problem solving. Problem solving is a hallmark of school leadership. Bringing in sensory data and picking up issues of sig-

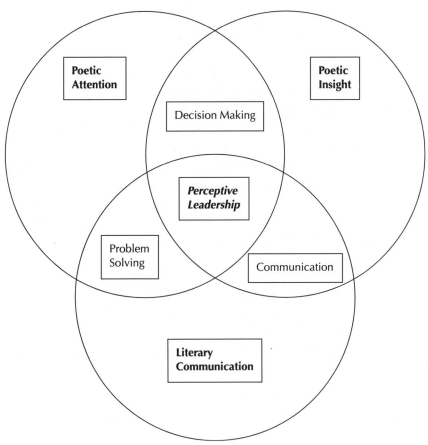

Figure 7.1.　The Perceptive Leadership Model

nificance from the environment allow one to better identify problems. Memory, imagination, intuition, and creativity are brought to bear on the problem-solving process, thereby enhancing the level of analysis.

Poetic Insight

Poetic insight has to do with cognition, new comprehension, development of understandings, and new meaning. It is the result of the poet's way of focusing intensely to discern what is of deep significance. This intensity of focus leads to deeper understanding where unfamiliar images become linked with familiar images, resulting in greater insight and creativity.

Poetic insight improves communication. Leaders with poetic insight are able to process the complexities of the environment with strategies that enable them to come to a deeper understanding of what they observe. They can then make decisions regarding how to frame the communication to create meaning for those they must lead.

By paying close attention when looking at the environment and in working with people, one is constantly picking up information of deep significance. This allows you to choose well what you communicate. This level of attention also allows you to decide how you would communicate, that is, the depth of meaning making that would be required based on the needs of the people you lead. Timing of communication is also important, and increasing the sources and kinds of data you pay attention to makes for more informed decision making. Communication becomes qualitatively different as you are better able to discern.

The new insights can then be brought to the decision-making process while looking at human and environmental needs. One can make qualitatively different decisions because this level of insight provides additional data. Combining sensory data with rational, logical data provides a perspective that enhances the quality of decision making as decisions are more closely linked to human needs.

Literary Communication

Literary communication refers to the poet's careful use of words to meaningfully express the insights gleaned from paying close attention. It is the poet's way of transmitting fresh insights and deeper meaning, the poet's way of mirroring life for the self and others to understand, relive, and enjoy.

Similarly, by using poetic sensibilities, school leaders can enhance problem solving by bringing in fresh insights and by framing and naming these new insights in terms that make the unfamiliar familiar and build bridges to understanding.

Perceptive leadership, then, is leadership that makes use of poetic attention, poetic insight, and literary communication, thereby using greater creativity and imagination in constructing meaning for themselves and for those they lead. To better understand perceptive practice, a few definitions must be clarified. These definitions are taken from the *American Heritage College Dictionary*, 3rd edition.

Percept is "the object of perception"; a mental impression of something perceived by the senses, viewed as the basic component in the formation of concepts; a sense datum. *Perceptible* means "capable of being perceived by the senses or the mind." Hence matters and issues in the environment are perceptible and provide sense data or perceptual data. *Perception* is "the process, act, or faculty of perceiving. The effect or product of perceiving. Recognition and interpretation of sensory stimuli based chiefly on memory. The neurological processes by which such recognition and interpretation are effected. Insight, intuition, or knowledge gained by perceiving. The capacity for such insight."

Perceptive is "having the ability to perceive; keen in discernment. Marked by discernment and understanding; sensitive." *Perceptual* means "of, based on, or involving perception."

Perceptive practice is practice that uses greater levels of recognition and interpretation, resulting in discernment, understanding, and sensitivity in one's work. Perceptive practice involves creativity, imagination, and memory. When one pays attention to precepts in the environment, one can use her imagination and memory to produce insights and knowledge from perceptual data. The resulting discernment is then to be communicated in ways that create meaning.

Perceptive practice requires the merging of insightful perception with the precise use of language to frame events, ideas, and goals, thereby communicating not only the facts but also feelings. In perceptive practice one observes not only the facts but also feelings; one listens for not only the facts but also for feelings; and one communicates not only facts but feelings. When followers believe that their leaders understand them, they are more likely to follow wholeheartedly.

It is important for leaders to mirror issues within and outside of the school with fresh insights. In this way those they lead can understand, derive meaning, and make sense of the information. Studying poetry trains one to observe keenly with the senses. One can learn to hear differences in sound and to see beauty in the commonplace.

Leaders must be able to discern how environmental changes will impact the organization. While knowing or understanding how past changes have impacted the school is important, the ability to perceive how future changes will impact the school is eminently more important, if one is to be proactive, to plan strategically, and to respond in ways that are best for the welfare of the schools and those who work in them. Projecting possibilities for the future is an important leadership task.

The future of public education requires new knowledge, new thinking, and new leadership to meet the emerging challenges as well as to maximize the opportunities the challenges present. To do that, and to do it well, requires exploring and examining new and creative ideas about what could enhance and possibly transform the profession. Put differently, we must be open to transcending traditional boundaries.

This work is an effort to help school leaders create meaning with the aid of the art and craft of poetry, so they are better able to "read" their environment, both external and internal, and to a greater degree tap into the resources within their reach. It is an effort to more fully explore and use the capabilities of the human mind to our advantage.

As we have seen in part 2, poetry has value that goes beyond stirring our emotions. Poetry gives us access to unique ways of viewing the world, of interpreting, analyzing, and communicating about the world. Poetry affords us the luxury of capturing our experiences in ways that can enhance perception by tapping creativity and imagination.

One can develop perceptive ability through the use of poetic attention, poetic insight, and literary communication. As we have seen earlier, poets scan the environment, paying attention to what is of significance, develop insights, and communicate them in deep, meaningful ways that touch the heart. Likewise, the perceptive school leader scans the environment, paying attention to what is significant, uses memory and imagination, develops insights, and communicates them in ways that create meaning, in ways that touch the hearts of those they lead. This means that the perceptive leader recognizes the poetry of school life, examines the story of school life, adopts the poetic mind-set, the poetic mood and spirit, and is therefore attentive and responsive to not only the facts but the feelings of those he or she leads.

Perceptive practice involves much more than simply thinking about what one should do next. It involves observing, analyzing, and proposing. In this sense, perceptive practice involves creativity in designing the possible future and courage to act, both of which can lead to significant self-development and organizational development. It involves focused attention, critical thinking, discerning, imagining, intuiting, and communicating. This means that the perceptive practitioner develops a sharp memory and vivid imagination and uses them in combination with well-chosen words to communicate in powerful ways.

Five steps to perceptive practice include:

1. Scanning the environment, both the internal and the external, for information that is of significance.
2. Paying attention to people and their needs.
3. Analyzing the perceptual data/using memory to bring to mind familiar issues and events that can connect to the new.
4. Discerning patterns/using imagination to link the familiar with the unfamiliar, creating new patterns, new insights, and knowledge.
5. Communicating with the appropriate words and emotions to convey the new insights persuasively.

An important aspect of perceptive practice involves paying attention to sense data or perceptual data. Perceptual data collection is not the same as scientific data collection. It has more to do with sensing, judgment, feeling, and intuition than with logic. Analyzing these data can add depth to understanding.

Perceptive practice is a form of professional artistry in which the practitioner focuses attention, gathers sense data, analyzes it to gain insights, and transforms the ordinary or matter-of-fact into the unusual or extraordinary. School leadership could be construed as partly an artistic act. The perceptive practitioner looks for features that dramatize the lives of people in schools. It is important to point out that this facet of leadership practice is not meant in any way to replace logical reasoning; rather, its purpose is to enhance that aspect of leadership.

Profound thought, active memory and associations, attention to hunches, imagining, seeing possibilities, discerning patterns, projecting future possibilities, constructing meaning, and gaining insights are critical elements of perceptive practice. So, too, are curiosity, interest, and open-mindedness. These elements are important for scanning the environment to find what is of significance, taking in information, and actively examining sense data.

For those who might be tempted to scoff at the idea of using the imagination or to question the value of perception, it might be helpful to remember that the idea of traveling by means other than horse and carriage was in someone's imagination not too long ago. In fact, the idea sprang from several people's imaginations. These people perceived the needs of the future, employed their creative imagination, and took action to meet those needs by bringing the idea of the motorcar to fruition.

THE NEED FOR PERCEPTIVE LEADERSHIP

Judging from the discussion of the context of schools in part 1 of this book, it is easy to understand why school leadership is not a role for the timid, or for anyone seeking a comfortable position. It is, today, a place for the brave, the competent, the tooled, the imaginative, and the adventurous. It is a role for those with drive, initiative, a strong spiritual core, and self-direction who are willing to take risks and to discover and even invent new and effective ways of leading. Leaders need the skills to analyze situations, interpret, and to think forward, and the courage to take action.

School leaders should have a sound rationale for why they are involved in this particular position. They must frequently remind themselves of what drew them into the profession in the first place. Extensive self-reflection and self-analysis are critical to effective school leadership. An important question for the school leader to consistently ask himself is, "How am I impacting others?"

Critically examining one's own behavior, beliefs, motivation, knowledge base, and impact on others helps leaders to be perceptive about their own behaviors and, consequently, about the behavior of their followers. In my estimation, leadership development is, first and foremost, self-development. The primary focus should be on one's own behavior. Leadership of the self precedes leadership of others. Perceptive thinking about one's own behavior and can significantly move one's leadership forward.

To move forward and to create new ways of doing things require speculations and judgments. Science advances through speculation and judgment. First, hypotheses are developed, then one sets out to prove them. Similarly, in perceptive thinking, when one discerns new patterns or develops new insights, one takes action based on the new knowledge. While it is vitally important to know what exists, to find what is possible takes a subtle shift in thinking. Perceptive practice in schools is about a different way of thinking—thinking forward based on discernment and new insights. It also involves a different way of being that results in greater inspiration.

The increasing environmental uncertainty demands that school leaders lead creatively and courageously; this requires a continuous ebb and flow between the leader's inner world of beliefs and assumptions and the outer world. It also requires that they share leadership as they make decisions and take actions that impact the lives of students, faculty, and staff.

SHARING LEADERSHIP

To share leadership well involves connecting with others in one accord, being of one heart and mind. But how are school leaders to attend to matters of the heart? While there are no quick, simple, or easy answers, the poet's craft, both process and product, may in some ways be useful. It could be argued that while the external environment is constantly changing, the basic needs of the human heart are constant. For this reason, appealing to the needs of the heart would be of inestimable value in most human relationships.

Essentially, school leaders must cultivate a network of relationships that support the work of schooling. The ability to do this well rests on the leader's openness to empowering others, which is contingent on the basic beliefs and assumptions that the leader holds about the people within the school.

Pellicer (1999) is convinced

> that our basic beliefs about people define the limits of their potential in the workplace. Our positive beliefs about the essential goodness of people gives those whom we lead the freedom to do great things; our negative beliefs predispose them to do awful things. Our basic beliefs about people encourage them to succeed on a grand scale or discourage them so that they fail miserably. Our beliefs about people give them license to become the best or the worst that they are capable of becoming. . . . How do you communicate those beliefs in an organizational setting? How many people in your organization are struggling every day as they try vainly to meet the

expectations attached to their work: What are you doing to help them in their attempts to do a good job? What are you willing to do? (28)

The willingness to share leadership is perhaps the most important facet of building a collaborative learning community. Of course, the level of one's willingness to share and the extent to which one will share leadership are contingent on the leader's perceptions of him- or herself and the beliefs he or she holds about others in the school.

Sharing leadership means giving others in the organization the opportunity to demonstrate what they can contribute, by involving them meaningfully in decision making. The perceptive leader is able to discern when others want to be involved in decision making. Perceptive leaders also recognize the importance of what to focus on, which, of course, indicates to those in the organization what is of importance. People care a great deal more about the decisions they make than they do about the decisions others make for them.

Precisely because the needs of the human heart are critical, to be effective, leaders must examine their motives, because human beings tend to be closely in tune with other people's motives. Most people are able to assess or perceive hidden agendas, smoke screens, inconsistencies, and the like. Genuineness is a prerequisite for sharing leadership. If the motives underlying the actions of leaders are perceived by others as being positive, then people will support leaders in their actions and assist them in their efforts to lead. On the other hand, if the motives underlying a leader's actions are judged by others to be negative, then people will resist those actions and challenge the authority of the leader at every opportunity.

In the midst of the complexity, ambiguity, and paradoxes of the environment in which they operate, school leaders must be mindful of the paramount need in those they lead for their leaders to be honest, genuine, and have the ability to "tell it like it is." In coping with ambiguity and complexity, leaders must make judgments and interpretations. In order to act courageously, leaders need to determine what information is available and what pieces of information are still needed. In other words, they need to figure out what is really happening, which takes a deeper level of perceptual thinking.

Perceptive thinking requires a pause to assess feelings, raise questions, take a positive look, consider alternatives, and summarize the big picture.

This pause allows for the processing of information, recognition of patterns, and building of perceptions. The practice of probing more deeply into situations can yield new insights. Like the poet, perceptive leaders recognize a pattern wherever they see it and translate their perceptions into a form of communication that will help create meaning for those they lead.

Perhaps we now need to awaken the poet within—that part of the human spirit that pays attention to the simple and seemingly mundane aspects of life. It is the part of the human spirit that can notice the pain in someone's eyes, the hurt in someone's heart, even the despair in someone else's soul. It is the very part of our being that is willfully stifled in order to get ahead, too focused to see, to listen, and to attend, that part of the human being that is not usually evaluated in an annual review, or looked at when considering promotion or tenure. Yet, it is that aspect of our humanity that attends, often fleetingly, to the deeper spiritual needs of those around us.

School leaders, by taking the poetic perspective, or awakening the poet within, can expand their ability to share leadership. As I see it, if one has a heart, one can lead, provided one is willing to connect with others in meaningful and purposeful ways. After all, everyone has a heart in the literal sense, and people tend to respond when the heart is touched. In essence, perceptive leadership is leading by the heart, leading from the heart, and leading with the heart, to connect with the hearts of others.

In our efforts to improve public schools, perhaps it is time to focus on the core of our humanity. Although changing curriculum, raising academic standards, and increasing accountability are important, in my view, the most vital reform is of ourselves, examining what we focus on as significant, what we believe about others, and subsequently how we respond to others.

A change in our attitudes and beliefs about what is important can radically transform schools in terms of how they are organized and how people in them work together to meet the needs of students and staff. Despite the intense efforts to restructure schools, it is common knowledge that the results have been disappointing. It is certainly not enough to change the way organizations are structured, or to raise standards and increase accountability. These efforts focus mainly on programs and practices. To attend more intently to people is a more complex undertaking, but a vital one, if the quality of education is to improve.

What are we willing to do? Are we willing to face ourselves and do what we know should be done? Do we have the courage to transcend traditional boundaries, or to return to basic truths at the core of human nature? Or do we continue to window dress the outside, leaving the inside untouched? The times in which we live demand this level of introspection and action.

We live in an age where everything is somewhat superficial. Notions of good and bad, of right and wrong, are changing, or are in a state of flux. We are drawn to the past because it has something to teach us. The past can enlighten us about the present and help us navigate the future. Poetry allows us to experience a strong spiritual connection to things around us and to the past. In the tapestry of life, poetry is one of the single longest threads to the past. As such it may have the most to teach us.

At a time when innovative thinking is a leadership imperative, several techniques of poetry can help leaders to think outside the box. We have to engage in the kind of scanning that allows us to broaden our perception and see our contexts and what the issues therein imply. For those overly concerned with the lack of precision in perceptive practice, remember that even scientists create hypotheses. They do actually speculate, all the time.

There is definitely a sense of pride and satisfaction when one creates something that is uniquely theirs, something that bears their personal signature. In schools, this would mean allowing people to use their creativity and contribute their insights to the creation of the school community. In sharing leadership, the formal leader allows for others to participate in and enjoy this sense of satisfaction and significance.

Invariably, there are people within schools who are willing to help solve some thorny problem but who are never enrolled in the process. They are never asked because they do not hold a leadership position. Human resources lie dormant in many schools. Real power in schools is about tapping into the wealth of human capital that exists there. It is about power over the self, power to control the self, power that goes beyond the self to others, allowing them to think, to create, to build the capacity, and to make a difference in their work. This sharing of power does not happen without courage and conscious action. The next chapter explores some ways in which school leaders can enrich school life and enroll others meaningfully, by leading with insight and attention.

Chapter Eight

Leading with Attention and Insight

Given the context in which schools operate, and the fact that human problems cannot be solved by the simple application of technical solutions, it behooves school leaders to make use of the poet's insight and powers of attention. Keeping in mind that poetry is also a way of looking at the world, this chapter explores how leaders can lead with attention and insight, by using the poet's eye to gather information from the environment, and by using the poet's mind-set in analyzing information. The third aspect of the poet's craft, the poet's pen, is discussed in the next chapter, which deals with communication.

In today's school environment, one can no longer passively follow procedures and guidelines. Rather, one has to come to terms with the complexity, variability, and uncertainty of work in schools and actively engage others in constructing solutions. School leaders must carefully consider their environment and their actions in order to gain insights. Unexamined experiences do not produce the insightful ideas that come when one reflects on, analyzes, and tries to make sense and meaning from those experiences. Attention and insight, hallmarks of the poet, are arguably required for effective leadership.

Common to most standards for school leaders today are the ability to manage information and resources, lead and connect people, understand the external context and increase student achievement. Each of these tasks of leadership could undoubtedly be enhanced by attention, insight, and effective communication. This is where the poet's willingness to examine what is happening, face the problems of life, interpret them, and discover the significance of common things can serve the school leader.

Without losing sight of reality, school leaders can sharpen their perceptive abilities to create a desired future. As it is with the poet, elevating the
human spirit is a task of the leader. The poet presents his or her material
intensely, in concentrated and heightened form to achieve the desired effect. One secret of the poetic mind-set is the ability to see the most ordinary events of life as interesting, to detect in ordinary routines that which
is beautiful and significant. Similarly, school leaders, like poets, must observe the events in their environment as interesting and seek out and recognize that which is beautiful and significant. To do this the school leader
would need to approach events with a sense of adventure, a sense that in
spite of surface appearances, this event could be interesting or significant,
rather than dull or routine.

As time goes on we see everything flowing away, and we begin to understand the charm inherent in the fleeting quality of our world. For example, in my youth I assumed only grandmothers grew old. My grand-
mother often warned me that youth and beauty fade away. At ten years of
age, I couldn't quite grasp that. Perhaps it was a lack of interest on my
part. Today, however, her trite saying holds a different level of significance and meaning. We witness daily the ephemeral quality of all life in
flowers that fade, seasons that change, hair that changes color, hair that
grows, hair that disappears, bodies that age. But what do grandmothers,
aging, changing seasons, and dying flowers have to do with school leadership? They point to the importance of paying attention.

In life it is incumbent on us to live the present to the fullest by seizing
the beauty in the things around us as they pass. So, too, the school leader
must pay attention to what is beautiful in schools and what is of educational significance in the external environment. In other words, in spite of
the complexity and the challenges, in order to make meaningful progress,
school leaders must choose how they pay attention. By using the poet's
eye, the school leader develops skills in keen observation, sensitivity, and
enhanced awareness.

It is time to consider other assumptions about school leadership to com-
plement what we already know and to make it effective for current and future needs. Being perceptive is not just reflecting, but being fully involved
in using creative imagination to identify and discern the deep-seated human needs of the present and those that are likely to surface in the near future. Leaders taking the poetic perspective analyze the context, attend to

human needs, and advocate for those they lead. The poetic leader communicates information with inspiration.

Poetry is complex, as is life and work in schools. This complexity requires some strategies through which to make sense of the environment. What I have sought to do so far, as shown in figure 7.1, is to separate and define three major aspects of poetry that hold great potential to enhance leadership. The separation of concepts is done purely for the purpose of facilitating discussion. The reader must keep in mind that attention, insight, and communication are interrelated and occur simultaneously. Table 8.1 attempts to provide further clarification.

Leaders can lead with attention and insight by using the poet's eye and the poet's mind-set in attending to human needs and by scanning the environment, as table 8.1 illustrates. Here the leader's attention is directed to focus on people, programs, and practices. Philosophy, culture, and human needs coexist in schools, creating a uniquely challenging environment.

The framework provides an understanding of people as needs-driven, programs as culturally driven, and practices as philosophically driven. I trust also that this framework allows the school leader to gain deeper insight beyond the surface of the people, programs, and practices.

The framework also presents three aspects of the poet's craft that can aid in sense making and meaning making. They can also help in decision making and problem solving by allowing a more insightful look at issues that surface in schools.

With the understanding that people are needs-driven, the leader can use the poet's mood and spirit to gain deeper insights into the human needs that surface. Knowing that many programs in schools are culturally driven, that they exist as a result of social, political, economic, or other forces in the existing culture, the school leader is in a better position to

Table 8.1.   The Poetic Attention/Insight Framework

Attention	Insight	Poetic Element
People	Needs-driven	Poet's mood/spirit
Programs	Culturally driven	Poet's eye
Practices	Philosophically driven	Poet's mind-set

seek out issues of deep cultural significance. The leader can use the poet's eye to scan the environment in ways that generate insightful data.

By understanding that practices in schools are largely philosophically driven, the school leader can use the poet's mind-set when problem solving or making decisions about methods of instruction, the nature and content of the curriculum, or other practices that are driven by deep-seated philosophical beliefs about the purpose of schooling.

This is neither a simple nor an easy task. Purposeful attention must be consciously practiced before it can become a habit. However, a critical first step is having a strategy for use in directing focus, analyzing situations, solving problems, and making decisions.

Three areas of significance are shown in table 8.1. One such area of focus is on people and their needs. Another is on programs and the sociocultural influences that drive them. The third area of significance is on practices and the philosophical beliefs that drive them. In the complexity of school life, this framework could be helpful in directing attention to what is of significance.

In managing a fast-paced, unpredictable, fragmented, and complex environment, effective leaders need to be analytical and perceptive about their work. Attention must be directed to what is important, and a tremendous amount of insight is required. Additionally, because of the enormous complexities of human organizations—the uncertainty, instability, and uniqueness that are commonly found in them—intuitive judgment and skill are vital. The insight column of the framework provides a direction for focus. However, the poetic elements can be used as tools to more effectively gather data.

A primary method of gathering information is to engage in environmental scanning. That school leaders need to speak and write effectively is readily apparent. What is not as apparent, however, is their need to be adept at scanning their environment and gaining insights before communicating. Ambiguity, uncertainty, and disorder are descriptors that come to mind as one considers the context in which school leaders work. It is, in a word, messy. Situations that require decisions are often fluid, difficult to analyze, and subject to any number of interpretations. The utility found in the poet's craft has the potential to improve a school leader's efforts at leading in such a context.

A major responsibility of school leaders in dealing with problems of the workplace is that they move from one problem to another, from one crisis to another, and one context to another with tremendous speed. In these brief, spontaneous interactions, information overload is par for the course. Events occur simultaneously, and leaders have to think on their feet. The ability to focus attention, analyze situations, recognize patterns, and interpret is paramount and must become second nature. While attention to the environment is important, attention to human needs is paramount.

ATTENTION TO HUMAN NEEDS

Attention to human needs is of primary importance in environmental scanning. As a matter of fact, it is the ultimate reason for engaging in the gathering of information. As one scans the external context, the information gathered is examined in light of its impact on those within the school. Similarly, gathering data regarding programs and practices in the internal environment is in the interest of meeting human needs as they are manifested in schools.

Perceptive leaders allow others to feel significant. To do so requires attention to their needs. The manner in which programs and practices are implemented impacts the level of significance that others feel.

Psychology tells us that human beings are motivated by need. Maslow's (1954) now commonly known hierarchy of needs groups human needs into five basic categories from lower to higher. The lower needs comprise physiological needs, safety needs, and belongingness and love needs. These lower needs dominate behavior when they are not satisfied.

The higher needs are considered as the need for esteem and for self-actualization. These higher needs become salient only after the lower needs have been satisfied. In schools, both lower and higher needs are manifested in staff and students on a daily basis. In order to meet the needs of those they lead, leaders must be able to discern which needs are dominating the behaviors they observe.

Oftentimes, how leaders respond or fail to respond to human needs results in resistance. When their needs are not being met, people sometimes adapt to the frustration by withdrawing physically, by being absent often, or by quitting. They may also withdraw psychologically by becoming indifferent, passive, and apathetic. This holds true for demotivated teachers as well as for students and other workers. Consequently, school leaders' ability to discern human needs and their willingness to meet those needs can make a difference in the culture that is cultivated with the school.

School leaders must pay acute attention to the level of congruence between the practices and programs and the needs of students, faculty, and staff. In schools, where change is constant, confusion and conflict are commonplace. People in schools are constantly taken out of their comfort zones due to changes in programs and practices. Perhaps it is accurate to say comfort zones no longer exist in schools. This draws attention to the critical role of leaders in orchestrating some level of congruence between human needs and their work.

Changes in practices and programs impact, often negatively, people's ability to perform their jobs confidently and successfully. This can leave them feeling inadequate and insecure. It is incumbent on the leader to find ways to assuage the intensity of this confusion, conflict, and sense of loss of competence experienced in times of change. It is the leader's role to cultivate an environment in which it is possible for those they lead to feel significant and experience some level of satisfaction.

Organizational performance, staff growth, and morale depend on responding to the needs and feelings of workers and on finding a good fit between their personal priorities and those of the organization. For the leader willing to pay attention to human needs, the focus here would be on people first, programs and practices second. In this situation the perceptive leader would take steps to make meanings clear, to uplift, and to ennoble.

To further emphasize the importance of a focus on human need as an area of prime significance in work, Marris's (1975) conceptualization of occupational identity elucidates the issue. Marris posits that each of us constructs an occupational identity based on accumulated wisdom— drawn from our own experience, that of colleagues, and lessons from predecessors about how to perform a job. However, change often discredits this experience, challenges our purposes and identities, and devalues our skills.

It is important to notice that the psychological reaction to change is such that it takes an insightful leader who is paying attention to discern the subtle shifts in posture toward work. Behavior and attitude shifts accompany even seemingly small changes in practices and school programs. The perceptive leader, by paying attention, can gain insights into the unmet needs as they are manifested and take steps to allay the situation.

Human need is at the core of this attempt to apply poetic lenses to the practice of school leadership. This effort to develop poetic sensibilities can sharpen school leaders' awareness of the manifold opportunities to connect at a deep and meaningful level with those they lead.

Perceptiveness directs the leader to the overall quality of life the staff and students are experiencing, as well as to areas of unmet need. Perceptiveness enables the leader to gather sense data in addition to scientific data. This combination of scientific data and sense data allows the school leader to make inferences, to gain new insights, and to get to understand the staff and students on a deeper level.

School leaders must be willing to look for what is unique about students and staff and connect to that. As Eisner (2002) points out, empathy, playfulness, surprise, ingenuity, curiosity, and individuality must count for something in schools that aim to contribute to a social democracy. These attributes come easier for some school leaders than others. When one is adept at self-leadership, it is easier to tolerate this level of artistry even when beset by challenges. Ironically, it is precisely when challenges are greatest that art may be most helpful, by bringing levity and creativity to an otherwise daunting situation.

A strong spiritual core enables leaders to be accessible to those they lead, particularly in times of crisis. Crises, small and large, dramatize the lives of school leaders on a daily basis. Most of the drama emanates from the nature of schooling. Understanding the politics, building support, and interacting with students, staff, and community call for a certain level of artistry in order to be done well. Perception plays an important role in art. So do open-mindedness, creativity, and levity. These attributes are accessible through the study of poetry and can contribute to the art of school leadership.

It would be helpful to keep in mind that while scientific theories are important, the human heart, intuition, and imagination may be infinitely more critical to school leadership. This view does not in any way preclude the use of concepts based in scientific research for school leadership. Theories about how schools work are important. Judgments have to be made and theories must be examined for their practical implications.

But, where science seeks to manage or control, art simply pays attention. Since one cannot control human behavior, but one can attend to human behavior, the notion of employing art should not seem too far-fetched.

Attention can result in influence on the behavior. By attending to and responding to human needs, one can better serve those they lead.

One cannot focus solely on what's measurable for one cannot measure creativity, imagination, passion, caring, love, or compassion. These are qualities that relate to the emotions, perceptions, and intuition. They are perceived by the heart rather than by the eye. It is critically important, then, that one should strive to inspire rather than control others. People must be inspired to perform. The leader's role is to inspire, and that is done by touching the heart.

Life is fluid, chaotic, and complex, and no simple procedure can tame it. This fluidity, chaos, and complexity are true in schools as in life itself. The uses of poetic processes presented here are not to be construed as a simple procedure to tame the chaos or complexity of schooling. Rather, the process of poetry has potential to help school leaders find what is significant, pay attention, develop insights, and communicate in ways that inspire those they lead to persevere in spite of the challenges they face.

The basic needs of the human heart are constant. People need to be loved, they need to be valued, and they need to be recognized for their efforts. This human need for belonging is universal.

As school leaders strive to pay attention to human needs, several questions raised by Sergiovanni (1999) may be instructive. These questions include: What can be done to increase the sense of kinship, neighborliness, and collegiality among the faculty of the school? How can the faculty become more of a professional community where everyone cares about each other and helps each other to grow, to learn together, and to lead together? What kinds of relationships need to be cultivated with parents that will enable them to be included in this emerging community? How can the web of relationships that exist among teachers and between teachers and students be defined so that they embody community? Taking the time to consider with faculty and staff the answers to questions such as these can enable school leaders to get a good sense of what the people they lead value and give insights into their needs. This is a critical part of scanning the internal environment.

USING THE POET'S EYE

It is important for school leaders to keep uppermost in their minds that schools are social institutions created by society to achieve socially defined purposes and as such they are subject by their very nature to influences from society. It is always amazing to me how surprised prospective school leaders are to hear this. Most have been working in schools for upward of ten years and have little understanding as to how powerfully context influences schools. A common sentiment in schools is, "If only the politics will just go away, we'll be fine." But public schooling is integrally linked to politics, and the leader plays a key role in helping those within schools to understand this aspect of schooling.

Influences in the larger external context often make demands on and generate certain types of behavior in the leader. We should not construe the school leader as this powerful person with power over the environment, since the environment has a tremendous impact on the school leader's behavior. By the same token, however, we should not construe the school leader as a person without any power to deal with the environment. Effective school leaders develop skills, abilities, and knowledge that enable them to work well with the contextual factors.

Schools are part of a much larger ecosystem. To be effective school leaders must study, understand, and use strategies to deal with the context. Not only are schools fiscally dependent on their communities, they are dependent on society for direction in what to teach, when to teach it, and how to teach it. Social forces, therefore, have an important effect on the climate within which schools operate. It is important for school leaders to understand this and not feel at the mercy of this larger system, but rather to develop the ability to scan and interpret the environment, analyze the information, communicate it to those who work within the school, and plan how to respond to these influences. In this way the school leader serves as a buffer between the society and the school. This is a vital role, which requires special skill to do it well, particularly since schools are impacted by contextual factors in ways that are not always obvious.

Poetic processes can be used to sharpen skills in observation, develop sensitivity, and develop the ability to focus on issues of significance. Among the various definitions of poetry is the following, which is particularly useful to this discussion:

> The poet's eye, in a frenzy rolling,
> Doth glance from heaven to earth, from earth to heaven;
> And as imagination bodies forth
> The forms of things unknown, the poet's pen

Turns them to shapes, and gives to airy nothings
A local habitation and a name.

—William Shakespeare

From the foregoing definition of poetry by Shakespeare we can readily glean some insights for school leadership. Poets, as Shakespeare sees them, are keenly observant. They survey, they examine, and they scrutinize the environment and use the imagination to make comparisons and connections. Then with carefully chosen words, the poet names or frames what has been observed so others can understand.

An apt and direct application can be made to schools today, where leaders are beset by problems of all sorts in a complex environment. School leaders need to survey the changing environment, identify the big picture by making comparisons and connections, and, with carefully chosen words, frame the external context for the school community in ways that make sense to them.

While conceptual ability and analytical skill are necessary for leadership, one must also have discernment and become perceptive in ways that will point to those things in the environment that are of significance to schools. Using the poet's eye to scan the environment and focus on issues of significance can be developed through practice or training that uses strategies to sharpen skills in observation, to develop sensitivity, and to focus closely on key details of significant issues.

These processes can also help to change attitudes toward the external context. Consequently, leaders must understand and strive to influence policy. In order to function effectively in schools, they need to understand the social and political worlds of education. School leaders must do more than observe politics; they must learn about and become advocates for current and emerging policies. It is vital today to increase one's knowledge of public policy and to enhance one's leadership skills in the policy arena.

By developing awareness and understanding of their social, political, cultural, economic, and technological worlds, school leaders increase their ability to scan the environment, interpret and analyze issues of educational significance, and communicate in ways that engender meaning to those within the school. Furthermore, the knowledge gained can provide information for improved decision making and problem solving.

By using the poet's eye, school leaders will collect information differently. They will use multiple sources of information. In so doing they broaden their knowledge base and enhance awareness of issues that can significantly impact schools. They are also better equipped to inspire those they lead.

To make sense of our experiences we usually construct patterns by connecting experiences. In some ways this mental patterning is a creative act of organizing our thoughts. This patterning is a vital aspect of perceptive leadership. As the external conditions change, the leader can connect experiences, construct patterns, and interpret the conditions to help those they lead make sense and meaning.

USING THE POET'S MIND

Essentially, leading is a creative act that involves the process of patterning or making connections and drawing comparisons to enhance reasoning. In advancing a theory of poetic thinking, Parker (1977) explains that the central activity in poetic thinking is metaphor making, or seeing, saying, and showing those compatible connections that we perceive to exist between various aspects of our experience. "These metaphors are not merely decorative in any sense. Rather, they provide the basic intellectual process by which man represents his experiences of the world, whether in images or in words" (11).

Using metaphorical thinking can aid understanding. In times of uncertainty, when situations are puzzling, school leaders can ask, "What can I liken this to?" By consciously and habitually engaging in making associative linkages, the school leader can develop strategies that can be applied in many different types of complex situations. Leaders can readily adapt some techniques of poetry to help them understand the array of human experience not satisfied by science. And poets seem to grasp this well.

Schools need to be led by creative, inspiring, and empowering people who pay attention to what is significant, interpret information, initiate conversations, and build relationships. School leaders must be people who are not afraid of innovation and risk taking that will meet the needs of those they lead.

Just as we do not expect artists to give psychological explanations for their effectiveness, so, too, we cannot expect to pin leadership down to a science. We must accept the fact that it is an art, and as such some aspects of it defy measurement and even explanation.

We learn in psychology 101 that humans are stimulus-seeking and pattern-forming organisms. Eisner (2002) believes that to make patterns well requires an environment supportive of exploratory thought that encourages people to entertain ideas in a spirit of tentativeness. Furthermore, Eisner argues for the importance of images and metaphors in shaping our conception of schooling.

These ideas are vital to my proposal here to broaden the base from which to view and practice school leadership. To meet the pattern-forming needs of others, school leaders must become adept at forming patterns themselves. This artistic side of leading school provides new knowledge and meaning.

By availing oneself of the poetic mind-set and the kinds of meanings it makes possible, a leader can unlock creativity, express feelings, and create images that can help ameliorate some of the strains and pressures in the everyday school setting. With greater use of the imagination in reading and interpreting the environment, leaders can better see the deep significance in issues that impact schools.

Using the poet's mind, school leaders can further develop the ability to analyze and interpret contextual issues that are critical to the success of schools. Specifically, they can learn effective ways to draw conclusions, pose questions, test answers, and make connections, thereby enhancing analytic skills.

The intelligence needed to create poetry can certainly be tapped and applied to the intelligence needed to create perceptive leadership. There is a limitation imposed when we seek leadership only through the lens of what is measurable. Unprecedented change as a result of technology, psychosocial needs of today's youth, and accountability demanded by the public demand new ways of leading.

The universality of change as the driving force in human affairs in our time requires greater emphasis on the soft side of leadership to help people through change. With the rise of school site management and the debureaucratization of school districts, many decisions must be made at the school level today, and they must be made quickly. This puts greater responsibility on the leader to be able to gather information and interpret it for those within schools.

It is important for school leaders to keep in mind that any power they hold is voluntarily granted by their followers. Leaders exercise power that followers have willingly entrusted to them. This power can only be maintained as long as the leader continues to keep them connected.

Cultivating Community

The idea of cultivating community carries with it a sense of caretaking as well as creativity. It indicates that deliberate actions are taken to help people feel connected and engaged in full, broad participation. The poetic mind-set of recognizing the significant in the ordinary and interconnectedness among things can be helpful in this endeavor.

Drawing attention to the universal reach of poetry, Skelton (1956) explains poetry as

> an incentive to further development and understanding of the total nature of life. It is based, always, upon a perception of the value of sympathetic and empathetic thinking, of the immense creativity of the sense of love. It is indeed, at all times, felt by the poet, not as an end, but as a purposive activity, and animated by a faith that the ultimate truth of existence, the essence of life, is somehow the existence within a continual experience of that activity, which is creative, unifying, dynamic, and ineffable. It is at once a patterning of the state of man, and an affirmation, in a series of deeply experienced realizations, of the persistent dynamic purposiveness of life. (197)

This universal reach of poetry, applied to school leadership, allows for expansion of ways of knowing, meaning making, and community building. Educational thought imbued with the poetic mind-set moves beyond nice slogans to dealing with some of the real problems that plague education. For example, the popular slogan "All children can learn" will take on a different meaning and result in different actions when examined and executed with the poetic mind-set.

Many schools today attest to belief or affirmation that all children can learn, but in reality respond quite differently to students who are not learning well. From a poetic perspective, these ordinary children can be seen for the miracles that they are. In short, they can be seen as extraordinary. They will be seen as young people equipped with some special gift or talent. In the same way the poet turns the ordinary, the dull, the routine into the extraordinary, the school leader creates a culture in which all children—especially average children—are seen as extraordinary. By being sensitively observant, the leader can discern talent and skill in the most average student. But the perceptive leader goes beyond observation. Imagination must be added to the observation so that a picture of who the child could become emerges.

The need for school leaders to cultivate community becomes urgent when we consider the realities of lives of children and their families and when we consider the implications of living the belief that all children can learn. Today not all children are fortunate enough to experience belonging to a family or receiving love from a family. At an earlier time we took these values for granted. Neighborhoods and families are not as secure as they once were. Children need a place to grow up, to play, to dream, and to interact positively with adults.

For millions of American children, the void is left to be filled by no other institution but the school. No other social agency has the kind of reach schools have to capture the hearts and minds of our young. School leaders need to find ways to attend to needs that children bring to school. This is not to minimize, in any way, the roles of the social worker, the psychologist, or the school nurse. But with increasing numbers of children needing these services, they cannot be relegated solely to these supportive structures. There must be built into the school itself, practices, and programs that can impact children's lives positively on an ongoing basis as they develop.

The internal environment of the school must be examined for the influence of the various interactions among the activities, physical environment, and norms of the school and their power to mold the behavior of the people in the school. When imagination is combined with observation, leadership becomes a creative act. School leaders can mitigate this influence by paying attention to the human needs and using the insights gained to guide changes in the type of community that exists within the school.

Community does not evolve on its own; the leader takes special actions to foster community. The poetic mind-set can be used effectively as a means of developing organizational learning or community learning, through attention and insight into human needs coupled with imagination and action. When people's needs are met, they are more willing to fully connect to others in the school. This spirit of cooperation and connection can and must be nurtured by the leader.

People, when motivated, are more likely to seek to satisfy their desire for belonging, connection, and love with others in their school community. Conversely, when demotivated, they withdraw as they seek to satisfy their desire for autonomy and self-reliance.

Understanding the value of cultivating community, perceptive leaders care about the people they lead and demonstrate genuine expressions of caring. Barring the initial clumsiness inherent in all new learning, a caring leader can naturally lead with poetic attention and insight. The ideas presented here are not meant to be used as gimmicks. Rather, they are presented with the intent of enhancing most of what effective leaders already do. For others, it is an invitation to explore different ways of finding and creating meaning in work.

One can learn to lead, and one can adapt to the structures and systems in a leadership position. However, caring comes directly from the heart, from who you are, and pervades what you do. How school leaders interact and the kinds of relationships they form greatly influence the kind of culture and community that develops, the quality of work produced, and the level of creativity and innovation that surfaces. Genuinely caring leadership brings out the best in those they lead. Followers tend to put more effort and energy into their work when they feel their needs are being met. Essentially, they bring their souls to work.

Engaging the Soul at Work

Until public schools hire chaplains (which is very unlikely), like some companies are now doing, the tasks of spiritual leadership rest with the school leader. Disheartened people are all too common in public schools. As possibly the last remaining social institution with a universal reach to impact children's futures, it would be to our detriment as a democracy to allow this disheartened state to perpetuate itself. School leaders must be in a position to inspire, ennoble, and lift the human spirit.

When needs are not being met, people become shortsighted, focused on themselves, and consequently ignore the organization. This leads to a dehumanized workplace where, to protect themselves, people go through the motions of everyday work devoid of zest for what they do. They seek to feed their hungry spirit elsewhere.

Most people want to be part of their organizations, agree Lewin and Regine (2000):

> they want to know the organization's purpose; they want to make a difference. When the individual soul is connected to the organization, people become connected to something deeper—the desire to contribute to a larger purpose, to feel they are part of a greater whole, a web of connection. When this context develops, people begin to openly acknowledge the need for others, to see their interdependence, and their desire to belong—their tribal instinct awakens. (27)

Herein is spelled out a critical task of school leadership: the ability and willingness to cultivate conditions that would address people's need for connection, to be part of something bigger that is aligned with their values.

This sense of shared purpose is cultivated by the leader. *Cultivated* is the appropriate word here, as the collective soul of the school community must be tended, like a garden, if it is to thrive. This means that what is valued must be protected from encroaching weeds and wild animals. It must also be watered and fertilized.

There are no simple solutions for engaging the soul at work. However, the leader's beliefs about people and what they are capable of could help or hinder their level of engagement. It is important to pay as much attention to how we treat people—coworkers, subordinates, customers—as we now typically pay to rules and regulations, structures and strategies, and protocol and procedures. Attending to the nature of the interactions within the school creates the potential for more humane connections and a school more effective in meeting human needs.

To engage the soul requires acknowledging that each person brings something of value to the school community. Furthermore, it means valuing what each person brings. It is to assume good intentions on their part. Of course, good intentions alone are not enough, but it predisposes the leader to act in a certain manner. It is in recognizing a job well done, not only with a paycheck but also with genuine appreciation. It is to believe in people and their potential rather than limiting them by tying them to their history. This perspective affects the quality of the interactions in a school and creates a positive boomerang effect of trust and commitment, rather than suspicion and disconnection. It is this boomerang effect that can transform the school.

To engage the soul at work is to focus not only on a plan of action but also to be alert to unfolding and unexpected directions and outcomes that are inherent in complex systems. It is to have a firm foundation of shared vision, values, and beliefs, yet maintain a level of flexibility to changes in programs and practices and a willingness to support people as they deal with change.

This means talking with people, listening to them, and responding in ways that help them feel supported, connected, and willing to bring their soul to their work. When people feel personally fulfilled at work, they are willing to contribute immeasurably to the school community.

A Culture of Care and Attention

Schools improve only when individuals that work and learn in them improve. Individuals tend to improve when they feel valued, when they feel a sense of belonging and a sense of fulfillment. This type of environment is characterized by trust, respect, support for innovation, and openness to new ideas. A culture of caring, sharing, and mutual help enables people to create and find meaning in their work.

Building a culture of attention, insight, and meaningful communication goes to the fundamental nature and core of our humanity. Leadership in a complex environment must be of a fundamental nature. It must be connected to what makes us human, and the poet's mind is attuned to what makes us human. Precisely because of the complexity of the school environment, leadership must be of the nature that resonates with the needs of the heart. In no small measure, leaders are called upon in times of crisis to bring hope in the face of despair and to genuinely nurture those they lead.

While crisis situations make this need more apparent, on a daily basis, students, faculty, and staff alike come to school dealing with their own individual crises and require some level of attention. Consequently, it is incumbent on school leaders to cultivate a culture that is keenly attuned to human needs.

This kind of culture can have a powerful effect on schools, fostering greater school effectiveness and productivity. A nurturing, caring culture can improve collaborative activities and facilitate better communication and problem-solving practices. Efforts at school change within a nurturing culture hold a greater chance for success. As this kind of culture takes hold, staff commitment is likely to increase.

By sharpening their skills in observation, school leaders can see past the overt behaviors as people respond to change. They are able to see the unmet needs. Whether the resistance is demonstrated overtly or covertly as fear and anxiety, or disregard and denial, the perceptive school leader takes steps to help those affected retain their sense of identity. The school leader helps them think about the circumstances differently in order to gain insight and make sense of the change.

A culture of care and attention amplifies the energy, motivation, and vitality of a school staff, students, and community. When the social climate is one in which people feel valued and cared about, it positively influences the emotional and psychological well-being of its staff and students.

Reducing the anxiety surrounding change and the fear of trying takes sensitivity to human emotion, a focus on people's needs, and communication that is framed in ways that bring meaning and sense to the situation. Even when people do not quite understand their needs cognitively, speaking to the heart tends to lessen the anxiety and allows the person to proceed to the cognitive understanding. The poet's ability to appeal to the heart is useful here. Likewise, to be effective with people in schools, leaders must be acutely aware of how they treat others each day and each moment.

This heightened level of sensitivity to others places certain demands on the character of the leader. Leaders cannot be preoccupied with their own self-interests. They must be committed to serve others in a very real sense. This means that one's own needs must be taken care of, as much as possible, prior to beginning the day at work. Leaders must be emotionally accessible to others. This kind of leadership requires leaders to develop certain self-renewal behaviors that will enable them to be available to and for those they lead. Care of the self, engenders care of others. This kind of leadership demands leading *with* both the head and the heart, *to* the head and the heart of those they lead.

In times of stress, leaders must connect to the heart first and the head later. At other times, the leaders use their best judgment as to the most prudent connection to make in order to get meaningful results. Depending on the situation, care and compassion may precede intellectual stimulation. An emotional response may supersede a rational one. Regardless of which is done first, this continuous dance between the head and the heart, between the emotion and the intellect, is at the core of successful leadership in a complex environment.

Since resistance is not only inevitable but an integral part of change, school leaders must become adept at this head and heart choreography. Meaning making is critical in times of change, and people come to meaning through the emotions first. However, one cannot rely solely on an emotional response to create effective change.

The leader, in times of challenging change, must step up both personal contact and information flow to help people see links between the new and the old. They need to understand that the future is not disconnected from the past and understand how they are related in significant ways. Consequently, the intellectual stimulation is as important as the emotional support.

This perspective focuses attention intentionally on people's needs. Care, empathy, and compassion create a climate in which people can trust and feel a sense of connection. An emphasis on goals, resources, efficiency, policies, and chain of command becomes secondary. In the midst of change, or at the onset of conflict, symbols are infinitely more important than rules. This is the time for the leader to resurface or create rituals, ceremonies, stories, or other symbolic forms that communicate hope.

One of the most significant roles of leaders is the creation and use of the symbols and symbolic activity that give meaning to the people within their organizations. When they cannot make sense of what is happening, people turn to the leader. How then shall one lead? When a leader has developed sensitivity to human need, it becomes infinitely more possible to uplift others in times of crisis. Followers require from their leaders both inspiration and information. Inspiration touches the heart, information, the head.

No longer can we ignore or avoid the spiritual aspects of leadership. After September 11, the importance of spiritual leadership was unveiled. School leaders had to make their words and actions meaningful to others. They had to find ways to uplift spirits. They had to help those they lead make sense of the crisis. They had to consciously and carefully choose words that brought comfort to hurting hearts. Addressing the needs of the human heart is how successful leadership is emerging at the dawn of the 21st century.

Cultivating a community that generates meaning, passion, and purpose on an ongoing basis creates a psychologically safe environment in which people can pour their hearts and souls into their everyday work. Thus, when crises occur, as they will, it is easier to attend to the heart and soul, rather than attempting, albeit awkwardly, to invite others to open their hearts and bring their souls to work unexpectedly.

To move from mere information to transformation, a leader must use communication that not only connects with the head but also with the heart. The Rev. Martin Luther King Jr., for example, is generally acknowledged as one of the great and powerful leaders of the 20th century. Dr. King had extraordinary power to influence the behavior of followers and ultimately the course of the nation. This stemmed from his ability to pay attention, gain insights, and communicate in ways that made sense and meaning to millions. His deftness at both communicating information and inspiring behavior led to transformation in the sense that people took action, and some even changed their behavior. He touched hearts as well as heads.

For while information is deciphered in the head, transformation takes place in the heart. Hence, we can glean much from the language of poetry to augment school leaders' ability to accomplish this task since poetry stirs an emotional response in the reader. When leaders set out to effect change, in addition to providing information, they need to provide inspiration by stirring an emotional response in their followers. This emotional response is vital, as it usually precedes action or change of behavior.

Providing information lets others know what you know, and others might respect you for your knowledge. However, it is in providing inspiration that others know how much you care. Invariably, inspiration leads to transformation. Just as great poetry moves us by touching our hearts, so, too, does great leadership. Great leaders inspire us, not merely through their level of knowledge, or their fine attire (though these could be impressive), but through their ability to touch our hearts and to move us to action. Just like great leaders, great poetry moves us with the same emotional appeal. Learning to lead well means learning to connect emotionally. And poets are masters of that craft.

Poetry serves to remind us of what truly matters in life. In destitute times we need to focus on what truly matters. Schools are ultimately about people—some who influence, some who supervise, some who teach, some who learn. Establishing and maintaining relationships among these groups are key roles of the school leader. What I am suggesting here is that the spiritual side of leadership must be emphasized in leadership preparation programs and validated and rewarded in practice.

Chapter Nine

Enhancing Communication

The effective use of oral and written language is a hallmark of leadership. Perceptive leaders, understanding the need for inspiration, share information with a freshness that is arresting to the audience. The school leader's ability to present a vision that audiences understand, feel connected to, and are willing to support determines to some extent the reach of his or her leadership. But successful communication as a school leader means a lot more than sharing a vision. It also involves the leader's ability to make requests in ways that validate others and the ability to mediate conflict in ways that leave others with their dignity intact.

Successful school leaders formulate and carry out plans for internal and external communications and build coalitions to gain financial and programmatic support for education. However, in all their planning and interactions, the focus is on how best to communicate in ways that meet the needs of others. This ability to communicate with followers is manifested in the narratives or stories a leader tells. The ability to tell the school story is vital to building support in the community. The ability to cultivate the school story is contingent on the quality of communication within the school.

Leaders in schools are charged with bringing unity out of diversity, and language plays a major role in that process. Consequently, skillfulness in communication is vital to a leader's success. Leaders strive to achieve order out of the chaos in the minds of those they lead. Choice words can serve to clarify otherwise confusing issues. Upon close examination of the poet's craft, one can see that things are made clearer by comparison and that poetic language often makes phrases more vivid and arresting than prose.

By virtue of their position, school leaders are looked upon as leaders in their communities. To be an effective leader, however, requires more than holding an organizational title. To lead well, one must be more than technically competent in planning, budgeting, curriculum design, scheduling, and facility renovation. One must be able to communicate with constituents, have something worthwhile and important to say to them, and be able to say it with a level of confidence that generates action.

Reading and reflecting on poetry can greatly influence a school leader's communication, both verbal and written. In addition to strengthening powers of insight and attention, the use of poetic technique can enhance communication, sharpen language, and stir one's own imagination to see above the day-to-day routines and perceive a grander mission that can ennoble the work. Poetry has the potential to allow a more careful examination of one's experiences, to encourage original thought, and to generate clear and effective communication.

Poets, in their communication, usually consider the spiritual aspect of being human by using symbols to stimulate, awaken, and deepen perception in the mind and heart. So, too, can leaders whose intent is to touch the human heart. To that end, the leader's posture toward life can make a difference. Examining the poet's mood and spirit may provide some insights into the mind-set that can continuously communicate to the human heart.

USING THE POET'S MOOD AND SPIRIT

Poets can change the everyday into the enchanting. While school leaders may not be concerned with enchantment, the need for transforming the dull and the routine into something more interesting is evident. For example, it can easily become routine to pass a class of students through four or five grades in a given school. Seeing each class, each student, each discipline problem with fresh eyes can illuminate the miracle each represents. The spirit of poetry instills a sense of awe into the everyday because poets are keenly observant.

Paying attention is the major means available to principals in communicating what they consider to be priorities. What leaders pay attention to is important for two critical reasons. First, what they pay attention to determines what becomes important and what is ultimately valued in the school. Second, what they pay attention to provides information for cultivating the symbolic life of the school.

For example, school leaders who make it a habit of consistently asking questions about achievement are probably more likely to see significant effort expended and subsequent gains in student achievement. Similarly, a school leader who consistently draws attention to the cleanliness of the school is likely to find others paying particular attention to the school's appearance. Where one allocates time, what one chooses to celebrate, and what one ceremonializes are the aspects of schooling deemed important. A leader should constantly ask, What do I consistently and persistently communicate? And how do I communicate those things?

The use of selective attention to signal important issues or events enables the school leader to focus attention and provide direction in solving problems. Selective attention also provides subtle bits of information that can be captured and symbolized or ritualized for effect. Take, for example, the senior slide experienced in most high schools, or the behavior changes exhibited by eight graders in a middle school. With careful attention, specific tasks of transition or leave-taking ceremonies can be developed to harness the energy, the restlessness, and the anxiety that tend to surface as discipline problems.

Leaders communicate their mood and spirit through their everyday attention. This attention is usually permeated with feelings that convey much meaning. Gestures, tone of voice, and facial expression of the leader transmit much more than mere words. It is essential for the school leader to be cognizant of body language. It is also essential to get a sense of who they are perceived to be by their audiences.

Questions in the minds of others regarding whether the speaker is trustworthy, has integrity, is knowledgeable, or is open-minded form a significant part of the communication they receive. This refers not just to surface image but to the substance behind the image. What one stands for and how one communicates these attributes are all part of the communication package.

USING THE POET'S VOICE

Poetry is not only a way of looking at the world but also a way of speaking about it. Using the poetic perspective to examine the environment is one way leaders can deepen perception. Speaking about the world of schooling metaphorically can help to deepen meaning and sense making.

Just as poets stand between us and nature, the school leader must stand between the external environment and the students, staff, and faculty. In that position, the leader as poet can communicate both to the rational and the emotional aspects of those they lead. School leaders can take advantage of the power of language to help create meaning. In looking at poetry, there is the idea, the meaning, and the theme. Similarly, leaders must focus clearly on the idea, the meaning, and the theme in framing communication. These aspects of poetry are infinitely more useful to school leaders than some other elements of poetry. While tone and imagery contribute to meaning, rhythm and rhyme might be less useful to the school leader. Although, if used judiciously, rhythm and rhyme can also be highly effective.

Listeners want stories they can relate to and understand, so leaders must call upon familiar signs and symbols as they communicate. Because audiences hear a lot of stories that compete with one another for their attention, the simpler the story, the more effective it is likely to be. Enhancing the stories with the use of condensed and emotive language can make them more effective meaning makers.

It is important for leaders to find their own voice. Otherwise, authenticity is diminished, and the leader ends up with a vocabulary that is not at all congruent with who he or she is. Exaggeration, dull phrases, or poorly chosen words do not make good poetry. Similarly, false expectations, unrealistic promises, disingenuous, dishonest claims reflect poorly on the leader. Natural, honest, forthright, heartfelt communication is best. It is important for school leaders to develop a superb command of language, to be able to use vivid, image-producing words, and maintain coherence and connection in speech. However, this is not to be done at the expense of losing meaning for their audiences.

Effective communication takes work. However, it is among the most valuable endeavors in which a leader can engage. Shaping one's ability to communicate effectively in a variety of situations goes a long way in the overall effectiveness in leading. Pointing to the importance of communication, Dyer and Carothers (2000) note that difficulties with communication account for many of the problems that are experienced by even the most seasoned educational leader. "It is not just what the leader says that determines facility in the skill of communication. It is also an ability to know what not to say and when not to say it that contributes to overall communication savvy" (27). This ability to know the *what* and the *when* of communication can be discerned through perceptive practice. Leaders can use a variety of techniques of poetry to help enhance skills in this area. Common forms of communication such as listening, speaking, writing, and silence can be sharpened by use of poetic techniques. The perceptive leader, with a focus on human needs, can communicate with the freshness and force of the poet.

With regard to listening, the perceptive leader understands that success in scanning and reading the environment is determined largely by the ability to hear not only the words but also the emotion that is being communicated through the tone, the imagery, the pace. In studying the poet's craft, one could become adept at phrasing language to communicate precisely what one wishes and simultaneously develop the ability to decipher the communications of others. Listening in perceptive leadership also involves the eye. The power of observation is critical here. One must observe with a keen eye the body language that accompanies the spoken work. Gestures, facial expressions, and posture may communicate intent more powerfully than the spoken word.

In speaking, the perceptive leader's focus is on meeting the needs of others. To that end, control of one's own emotion is as important as designing communication to evoke specific emotion in others. Hence, one examines his or her verbal communication for emotional content. This does not mean that leaders deliver their speech without emotion, but that the emotion is intentional, carefully chosen for impact or effect. The poet's mood and spirit are frequently conveyed through the emotional content of a poem.

Similar to the spoken work, the written word must be carefully crafted to inform and inspire. Poets are masters in the use of condensed, effective, and emotive language. Specific strategies for expressing ideas with sensitivity to human needs can be gleaned from the craft of poetry. In working to enhance school leaders' ability to better use contextual information in decision making, problem solving, and communication, an examination of the poet's pen may prove useful.

An essential and frequently underused aspect of communication is silence. School leaders may also benefit from observing that poets leave some things unsaid. Silence may communicate any number of messages. It is also important to watch for the body language that accompanies the silence.

The perceptive leader, like the poet, reads environmental clues to determine when silence is the best form through which to communicate what has to be said. Alternative choices may be economical and judicious use of words or a more liberal use of words punctuated by moments of silence. In many cases what is left unsaid is as important as what is said. Effective communicators, like poets, are selective in what they choose to communicate verbally and in writing.

Communication is much more than verbalizing words, even the right words. It involves one's whole being. And the major goal is to engage others and connect with them in ways that uplift, give hope, and move them to action.

Facts alone do not persuade others. In an increasingly diverse culture, it becomes more challenging to find common ground apart from the core aspect of human existence. And this is precisely where the perceptive leader directs communication—to the core of one's humanity.

To move people to action requires a level of authenticity on the part of the leader and the ability to connect emotionally to the audience. Sincerity, honesty, and passion must be transferred in the process of communication. People are emotional first, rational second. Consequently, the leader must connect to the heart first, the head second.

The social organizational realities of a school demand not only effective interpersonal skills but also strong intrapersonal skills. The intrapersonal comprises knowledge of oneself and one's skills, personality, talents, emotions, goals, and needs. On a practical level, high visibility is inherent in the position of school leadership. The need to use effective communication skills; the ability to resolve conflict; the abilities to treat individuals with fairness, dignity, respect, and to recognize a variety of ideas, values, and cultures call forth the best one has to give of oneself in service. To do this well, however, one must be in touch with the authentic self, that is, knowing who one is, what one stands for, and what one really cares about. This generates a level of congruence between what one says and what one does. It also helps determine one's own voice. The level of enthusiasm, energy, and passion conveyed by leaders makes a difference in whether they are heard or understood, and whether people who listen are inspired or left unmoved.

Attention to the fears, hopes, and dreams—the stuff common to the human heart—makes transformative communication work. Honest, sincere, and authentic communication builds trust and credibility. Facts alone never really leave any lasting excitement. Facts do not carry the persuasive power of emotive language. Some good news may energize initially, but building and sustaining momentum takes much more than facts. It takes enthusiasm, energy, and commitment even in the face of odds. It requires that the leader demonstrate behaviors that help take people to places they have not yet been and to achieve what they thought was not possible.

USING THE POET'S PEN

In writing, as in speech, choice of words is critical. The ability to stir an emotional response through the written word is vital to a leader's communication. This is where the poet's skill in choosing words can be helpful. Of course, the use of precise language is likely to be mechanical and pretentious unless it results from attention to issues of significance and from insights into the needs and feelings of others. Intense focus and attention, when coupled with the sense data derived from insights into needs and feelings, provide information, which when communicated through skillful and precise use of language, can resonate with others. Leaders' use of condensed language and inspirational words can be effective in an environment in which time is at an absolute premium, where activities constantly overlap one another, and where leaders navigate through several unfinished events simultaneously. The use of metaphors and similes effectively connects the familiar with the unfamiliar, provides fresh insights, and stimulates creativity.

This creativity is greatly enhanced by attention and use of the imagination. Paying attention to message and intent allows leaders to craft their language so it resonates with the reader. Just like poets, because of the irreversible nature of communication, school leaders must be concerned with language and its use.

A brief examination of some techniques of poetry can elucidate ways in which the process of poetry may be useful to school leaders. Simplicity, appropriateness, restraint, economy, and accuracy have been identified by several writers, including Walter (1962), as common techniques used by poets. These as well as a few additional techniques of poetry, such as imagery, refrain, and rhythm, will be examined for usefulness to the school leader.

Simplicity

A poet searches for the right words not only to express his or her exact meaning, but also to arouse the imaginative, emotional, and intellectual response of the reader. Simplicity addresses the need for understanding by the reader. School leaders should not let the search for imaginative words lead them to adopt euphemisms and artificial expressions that cloud clarity or are likely to preclude them from being taken seriously. They must search for the words to convey ideas in a straightforward manner, simply and directly.

Appropriateness

In poetry, appropriateness is the ability to say the right thing at the right time, to choose words that suit the mood, the emotion, and the thought. This can be accomplished by the development of one's vocabulary, careful consideration of the needs of the audience and the context in which the message is to be delivered, and revision of one's communications. Reading poetry can serve to stimulate creative uses of language.

Restraint

The necessity of being selective rather than giving in to the need to tell all is referred to as restraint. This technique gives added significance to language. It also gives value to spoken or written communication. The tendency to tell all could be fatal to a leader. Just as the best poems are weakened by "laying it on too thick," or by vulgar language, so, too, is the communication of a leader of a complex organization. Talking too much can be ineffective. It can aggravate others.

Restraint also includes the ability to avoid engaging in things like name-calling or other antagonizing communication such as violent language, vulgarity, or profanity.

Economy

The technique of economy is quite similar to restraint, except that in this case it has to do with the number of words rather than the kinds of words. Wordiness is not usually a hallmark of poetry. Poets say what they have to say briefly and forcefully.

The pace is fast in schools, and there is no time for long-winded leaders who take five pages to expound an idea that could well be expressed in one, or who takes two hours to communicate an idea that could be concisely and effectively done in thirty minutes. A school leader, to be effective, cannot afford to send memos that are full of careless repetitions, pointless musings, and unnecessary ruminations.

A critical part of school leadership preparation should be learning to eliminate weak words, unnecessary words, and words that add nothing to their communication. Prospective school leaders require practice in using words that mean exactly what they want to say and do not require an overabundance of additional phrases to explain them.

Accuracy

Working in tandem with economy is accuracy. Poets achieve accuracy not by adding all the words that could possibly be used in one connection, but by searching until they find the exact word or phrase to express their meaning, a colorful word or phrase that fits into the pattern.

While school leaders do not want to be overly colorful, prudent use of interesting or uncommon words can be effective in connecting with the right brain and conveying meaning readily. Good diction means not only accuracy in word choice, but also accuracy in word usage and correct grammar. These, too, are important for the school leader.

A poet searches for the right words not only to express exact meaning, but also to arouse the imaginative, emotional, and intellectual response of the reader. The poet uses not only the significant, accurate word, but the word which at the same time presents the best picture and stirs in the reader an emotional appreciation of the poet's mood and idea.

Imagery

Imagery is the basis of the language of imagination. In poetry imagery presents a mental picture of an idea through sensory appeal, connotative language, and comparison. This helps to evaluate the unknown in terms of the known and in expressing likeness in objects that are quite different. Imagery gives concreteness to abstract ideas and perception. Imagery, then, can be used effectively by the leader to show connections among disparate aspects of their complex environment.

Additionally, poets examine their work for harsh sounds and phrases unsuitable for an idea and substitute sounds and phrases that are appropriated to the mood and meaning they are trying to portray. They select words with accents properly placed to fit into the rhythmic pattern and make intelligent use of alliteration, assonance, rhyme, and cadence. In this way they add to the artistic significance of their work.

Just like poets who are constantly searching for resemblances in things that are quite different and express them metaphorically, school leaders can use the poet's eye to scan the changing environment, gain insights, and, with carefully chosen words, communicate to the school community in ways that will help to make sense of the information.

Refrain

Interestingly enough, refrains may at times be judicious choices for leaders in their communication. A refrain is a chorus, a phrase, or a few lines repeated in a poem. This brings to mind Dr. King's famous "I have a dream" speech. In that speech, the refrain served to make the speech more effective, pungent, memorable, and moving. While this should not be overdone, selective use of refrain can certainly enhance a leader's verbal communication.

Rhythm

Another seemingly unlikely but useful tool of the poet is rhythm. Rhythm is a measure of movement by regular recurring accents. One can readily observe the rhythms of life in the ebb and flow of the tides, the regular progression of day and night, the ordered march of the seasons, even the breathing of the body and the throbbing of the heart.

Rhythm, then, is as natural to us as breathing. Applied to school leadership, this does not mean leaders should speak or write in rhythms, but that they should, in examining the environment, look for patterns and recurring themes and point them out in their communication with the school community.

Used judiciously, these techniques of poetry can make communication vivid, memorable, and meaningful.

Table 9.1 shows a professional development framework designed to help school leaders develop poetic sensibilities.

The framework focuses on developing or enhancing poetic sensibilities in attention, insight, and communication. Developmental experiences are focused on three areas of poetic skill: Attention, insight, and communication, each aligned with corresponding skills to be enhanced or developed and use of those skills. These developmental experiences can be conducted through seminars, workshops, and on the job assignments. Of course, openness to the idea of using poetry and motivation to learn would be important elements in success with this type of professional development.

In addition to the developmental experiences and the motivation to learn, it is important that organizational structures support rather than hinder this type of professional development. To that end, it would be advisable that whole school staffs be trained together in order to foster broad understanding of the skills, so that leaders are not suddenly using metaphorical speech to which others can make no connection or meaning. A basic full-staff development training centered on the needs of people in schools and ways in which they can be attended to through

Table 9.1. Professional Development Framework

Poetic Sensibility	Skill	Use	Experiences
Attention	Observation	Environmental scanning; identifying the big picture	Reflecting and analyzing to come to terms with complexity. Going beyond usual ways of viewing problems; collecting perceptive data. Seeing beyond day-to-day routine
Insight	Imagination and memory	Making comparisons and connections	Metaphorical thinking, synthesizing. Discerning and making connections, bridging familiar to unfamiliar, perceiving new and different possibilities
Communication	Writing and speaking	Choosing words to engender meaning	Reading, writing, and examining poetry to develop or enhance speech and writing

communication can help in laying the groundwork for some level of institutional support.

School leaders need additional role-specific training designed for refining and sustaining poetic sensibilities. Like all communication skills, if not practiced they are likely to be lost. To be sustained, organizational supports for continuous learning must be in place, and new ways of thinking must be honored.

It is certainly understandable that many school leaders may not be familiar with poetry, may feel anxious about poetry, or even feel uncomfortable with poetry. Some might even question its academic legitimacy and be much more willing to settle for knowledge about poetry rather than the experience of poetry. The developmental experiences are to be structured to address different levels of motivation. For example, some school leaders might initially engage in either listening to poetry or reading poetry. Others might choose to do both. Still others might want in-depth study or might be ready to engage in writing poetry.

Ultimately, however, this professional development is not about poetry. Rather, it is about ways of enhancing or developing new skills that will help leaders in their challenging tasks of running schools and in becoming more attentive to and insightful about human needs as they present themselves in the school setting. It is also about how leaders communicate in ways that engender meaning for those they lead.

I am not advocating how to read, write, study, or critique poetry for the sake of doing so. Rather, I am concerned with using the process of poetry as a way of looking at the world and a way of discovering new connections, about uncovering at a deeper level what makes us human and attending to that unity. The ideas here are about developing enhanced insight, critical thinking, and meaning making, going beyond analysis to synthesis. They speak to the need for leaders to examine the lenses through which they view the world to discover its vibrancy and beauty.

This framework is proposed with the foregoing in mind and with the understanding that a critical need exists to provide a sound rationale for legitimizing poetry as a form of leadership development. In no way is the use of poetry meant to be construed as a silver bullet. It can, however, bring some levity to an otherwise increasingly daunting role, put things in a new light, stimulate the flow of interesting or provocative ideas, foster divergent thinking and creativity, and generate deeper levels of meaning in school work. School leadership is not in such an advanced state of development that it should ignore attempts to improve it.

In answer to Hölderlin's question, "What are poets for in a destitute time?" I answer with a quote from Untermeyer et al. (1938): "A good poem can not only help, but heal; it is an antidote against gloom, a mental and spiritual medicine" (447). In destitute times poets not only help, they heal, they become an antidote against gloom and despair; they become mental and spiritual medicine—the same role school leaders are called to play in our present age.

Chapter Ten

Epilogue

Leaders today cannot afford the luxury of silence about the spiritual condition of our places of work. As the stress mounts, leaders find themselves coping with their own stress as well as that of their organizations. The spiritual condition of an organization is as important as the roles, tasks, and structures therein.

A body without spirit is dead. Similarly, a body of people without a spiritual core is dead. People go through their daily routines with no inspiration. Their hearts and souls are not invited into their workplace. It is incumbent on leaders of all organizations to attend to the spiritual aspects of the workplace. In schools where young minds are being developed, there is a more urgent need.

Since what goes on in the spirit affects one's work, spiritual barrenness in faculty and staff is likely to impact students. Moxley (2000) understood this well when he pointed out that most of us are only dimly aware of how what goes on deep inside affects our involvement, for good or bad, in leadership activities. He sees inner life and outer work as inextricably linked and points out further, "What you see is not all of what you get. Unwittingly and unintentionally, we project what goes on in our depths onto all of our outer experiences, including our practices of leadership. What we project is not always benign; sometimes it is toxic—to ourselves, to others, and to our organizations" (130).

Leaders today must be committed to developing norms whereby those within their organizations can bring their whole selves to work. A spiritually dead school could be ignited by the passion of a perceptive leader—one perceptive enough to see the unmet human needs and take steps to ignite or rekindle the spirit by reaching out and touching the hearts of those they lead. In the long run, it does not really matter how much effort is put into the outer trappings of schooling if the spiritual core is dead or dormant.

The needs of the human heart have been underemphasized in the literature on leadership. One of the main points of this work is to posit that a core function of leadership is to make sense and meaning for those they lead. And that is done primarily by addressing the needs of the human heart.

In light of the widespread consensus that America's schools need significant improvement, we should explore all feasible options, particularly those that focus on unmet human needs. The fact that schools are primarily about people should point us in a certain direction. That direction points toward attending to the real needs of people.

Like Sergiovanni (1999) I agree that we should be blunt about the spiritual nature of leadership; "we cannot achieve community unless we commit ourselves to the principle 'love they neighbor as thyself'" (138). This ability to build community in schools is ultimately what poetic sensibilities attend to. Poets influence what and how we think. They draw our attention to certain things, amplify others, and recast many aspects of our lives with freshness, force, and intrigue. By virtue of their work, school leaders are called to be engaged in the same kind of work.

The slippery concept of spiritual leadership should not deter the nonreligious, since this is not about religion, but about attending to what makes each of us human. My purpose here is to help school leaders find additional ways to meet the challenge and struggles inherent in building community within schools by attending purposefully to human needs.

In challenging times, the main role of leaders is to offer hope and to instill faith, by leading with the heart. There are many ways to excel in leadership. Yet, at the core of leading schools well is attention to the needs of children and the needs of faculty and staff, as they seek opportunities for growth and recognition for their work. The awareness of something grander and more important than individual success is part of what gives them hope.

The suggestions presented in this book are neither tricks of poetry nor panacea for what ails schools. This work is intended to raise awareness of the need to attend more closely to what makes us human and in so doing provide an environment in which the human spirit and soul can thrive in the daily work of schooling.

This idea is not necessarily far-fetched. Our world needs more people who are not afraid of new or different ideas, people who are willing to evaluate them and apply them as possible solutions to some of our common problems. The high levels of interaction make schools unique organizations. The leader's task of connecting with the head and the heart is of infinite value. While not prescriptive, the craft of poetry can certainly help in this task. An essential need of growing and developing human beings is attention, and poets are masterful in their ability to pay attention.

I implore the reader to avoid taking a one-sided view of poetry, but rather to strive to see both the qualities of the poetic spirit as well as the qualities of poetry. It has been said that there is a poet in everyone. My hope is that readers will not only explore the value of the poet within, but make use of it to benefit themselves and others.

References

Altenbernd, L., and L. Lewis. 1966. *A handbook for the study of poetry*. New York: Macmillan.

Bolman, L. G., and T. E. Deal. 1991. *Reframing organizations: Artistry, choice, and leadership*. San Francisco: Jossey Bass.

——. 1995. *Leading with soul: An uncommon journey of spirit*. San Francisco: Jossey-Bass.

——. Leading with soul and spirit. *The School Administrator* (2) 59 (February 2002): 21–26.

Briskin, A. 1996. *The stirring of the soul in the workplace*. San Francisco: Jossey-Bass.

Brooks, C., and R. P. Warren. 1965. *Understanding Poetry*. 3rd ed. New York: Holt, Rinehart, and Winston.

Deal, T. E., and K. D. Peterson. 1999. *Shaping school culture*. San Francisco: Jossey-Bass.

Donaldson, G. A. 2001. *Cultivating leadership in schools*. New York: Teachers College Press.

DuFour, R. 1998. *The principal series: Facilitator's guide*. Alexandria, Va.: Association of Supervision and Curriculum Development.

Dyer, K. M., and J. Carothers. 2000. *The intuitive principal*. Thousand Oaks, Calif.: Corwin Press.

Eisner, E. W. 2002. *The educational imagination: On the design and evaluation of school programs*. Upper Saddle River, N.Y.: Prentice Hall.

Eliot, T. S. 1933. *The use of poetry and the use of criticism*. London: Faber and Faber.

Geballe, S., and D. Hall. 2001. *The state of working Connecticut 2001*. New Haven, Conn.: Connecticut Voices for Children and the Economic Policy Institute.

Geertz, C. M. 1973. *The interpretation of cultures.* New York: Basic.

Gioia, D. 1992. *Can poetry matter? Essays on poetry and American culture.* Saint Paul, Minn.: Graywolf Press.

Hillyer, R. 1960. *In pursuit of poetry.* New York: McGraw-Hill.

Hirsch, E. 1999. *How to read a poem.* New York: Harcourt Brace.

Hoyle, J. R. 1995. *Leadership and futuring.* Thousand Oaks, Calif.: Corwin Press.

———. 2002. *Leadership and the force of love: Six keys to motivating with love.* Thousand Oaks, Calif.: Corwin Press.

Jerome, J. 1984. *On being a poet.* Cincinnati, Ohio: Writer's Digest Books.

Kouzes, J. M., and B. Z. Posner. 1999. *Encouraging the heart: A leader's guide to rewarding and recognizing others.* San Francisco: Jossey-Bass.

Lane, R. E. 2002. *The loss of happiness in market democracies.* New Haven, Conn.: Yale University Press.

Lawler, E. E. 2001. The era of human capital has finally arrived. In W. Bennis, G. M. Spreitzer, and T. G. Cummings, eds., *The future of leadership* (pp. 14–25). San Francisco: Jossey-Bass.

Lewin, R., and B. Regine. 2000. *The soul at work: Listen, respond, let go: Embracing complexity science for business success.* New York: Simon & Schuster.

Marris, P. 1975. *Loss and change.* Garden City, N.Y.: Anchor Books.

Maslow, A. H. 1954. *Motivation and personality.* New York: Harper.

Maurer, M. M., and G. S. Davidson. 1998. *Leadership in instructional technology.* Upper Saddle River, N.J.: Prentice-Hall.

Moxley, R. S. 2000. *Leadership and spirit: Breathing new vitality and energy into individuals and organizations.* San Franciso: Jossey-Bass.

National Policy Board for Educational Administrators for the Educational Leadership Constituent Council. 1995. NCATE program standards.

Owens, R. G. 2001. *Organizational behavior in education.* 7th ed. Needham Heights, Mass.: Allyn and Bacon.

Parker, R. P. 1977. Poetic writing and thinking. (Report prepared at Rutgers, The State University.) ERIC Document Reproduction Service No. ED 136 258.

Pellicer, L. O. 1999. *Caring enough to lead.* Thousand Oaks, Calif.: Corwin Press.

Plsek, P. E., and T. Greenhalgh. Complexity science: The challenge of complexity in healthcare. *British Medical Journal* (323) 7313 (September 2001): 625.

Rodriguez, A., ed. 2001. *Essays on communication and spirituality.* Lanham, Md.: University Press of America.

Rollins, W. G. 1983. *Jung and the Bible.* Atlanta, Ga.: Knox Press.

Sergiovanni, T. J. 1992. *Moral leadership: Getting to the heart of school improvement.* San Francisco: Jossey-Bass.

————. 1996. *Leadership for the schoolhouse: How is it different? Why is it important?* San Francisco: Jossey-Bass.

————. 1999. *Rethinking leadership.* Arlington Heights, Ill.: Skylight Training and Publishing.

Skelton, R. 1956. *The poetic pattern.* London: Routledge and Kegan Paul.

Stauffer, D. A. 1946. *The nature of poetry.* New York: W. W. Norton.

The Task Force on School District Leadership. February 2001. *Leadership for student learning: Restructuring school district leadership.* Washington, D.C.: Institute for Educational Leadership.

Untermeyer, L. 1926. *The forms of poetry.* New York: Harcourt, Brace & World.

Untermeyer, L., Ward, B. E., and R. Stauffer. 1938. *Doorways to poetry.* New York: Harcourt, Brace & World.

Vail, P. 1998. *Spirited leading and learning.* San Francisco: Jossey-Bass.

Walter, N. W. 1962. *Let them write poetry.* New York: Holt, Rinehart, and Winston.

Watts, C. Bread and wine (after Hölderlin). *Chicago Review* (39) 3/4: 133.

Wheatley, M. 1999. Good-bye, command and control. In F. Hesselbein and P. Cohen, eds., *Leader to leader* (pp. 151–168). San Francisco: Jossey-Bass.

Index

*Italic numerals indicate tables.

About the Author

Lystra M. Richardson is an associate professor in the Department of Educational Leadership and coordinator of the sixth-year and certification programs in educational leadership at Southern Connecticut State University. She previously served as a central office administrator and language arts teacher for the New Haven Public Schools and as an implementation coordinator for the School Development Program at Yale University.

Her areas of specialty are curriculum, supervision, organizational behavior, and school leadership. Her research focuses primarily on school leadership. Dr. Richardson has published articles in peer-reviewed educational journals.